HMS INVINCIBLE

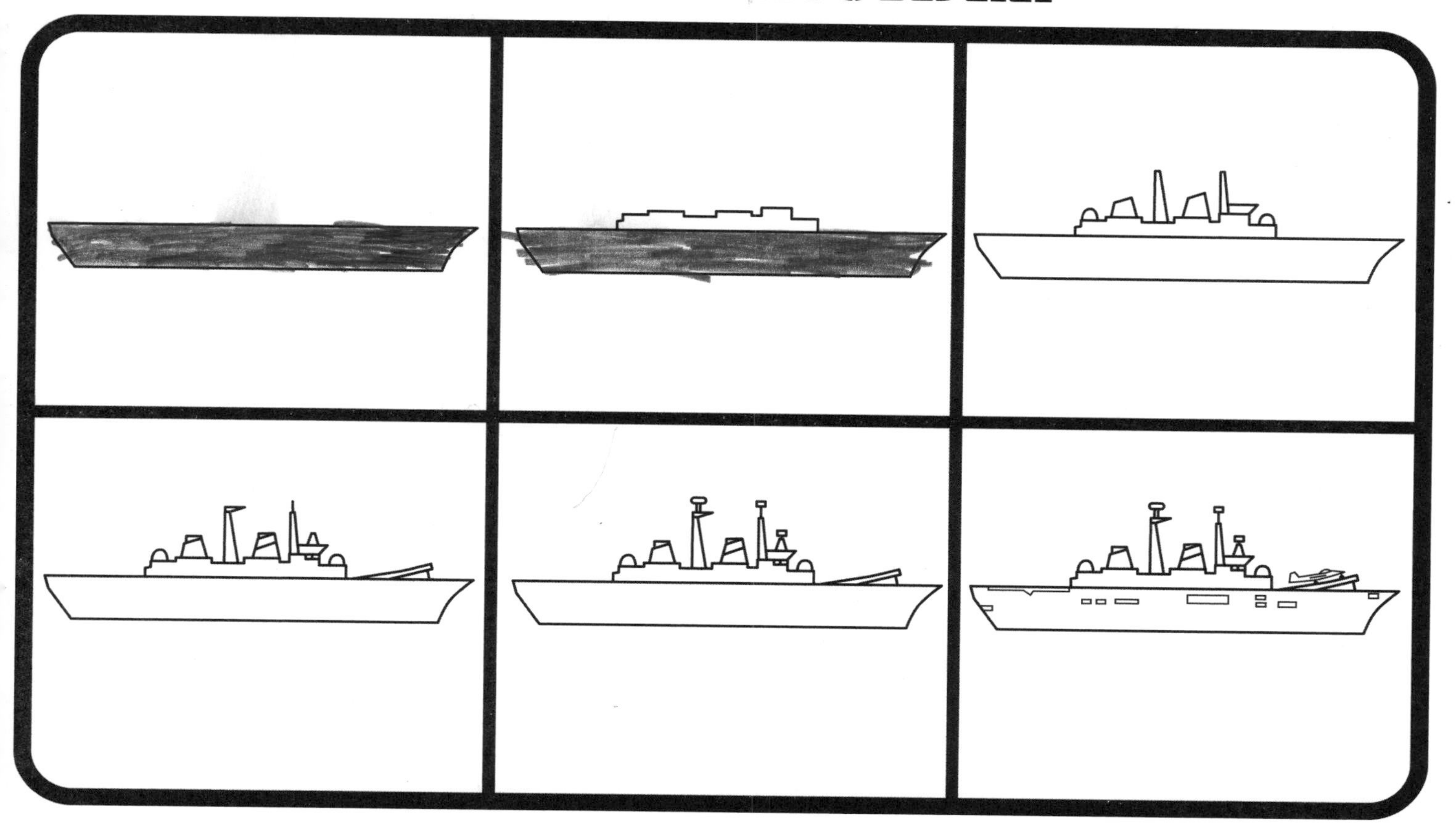

USS WASP

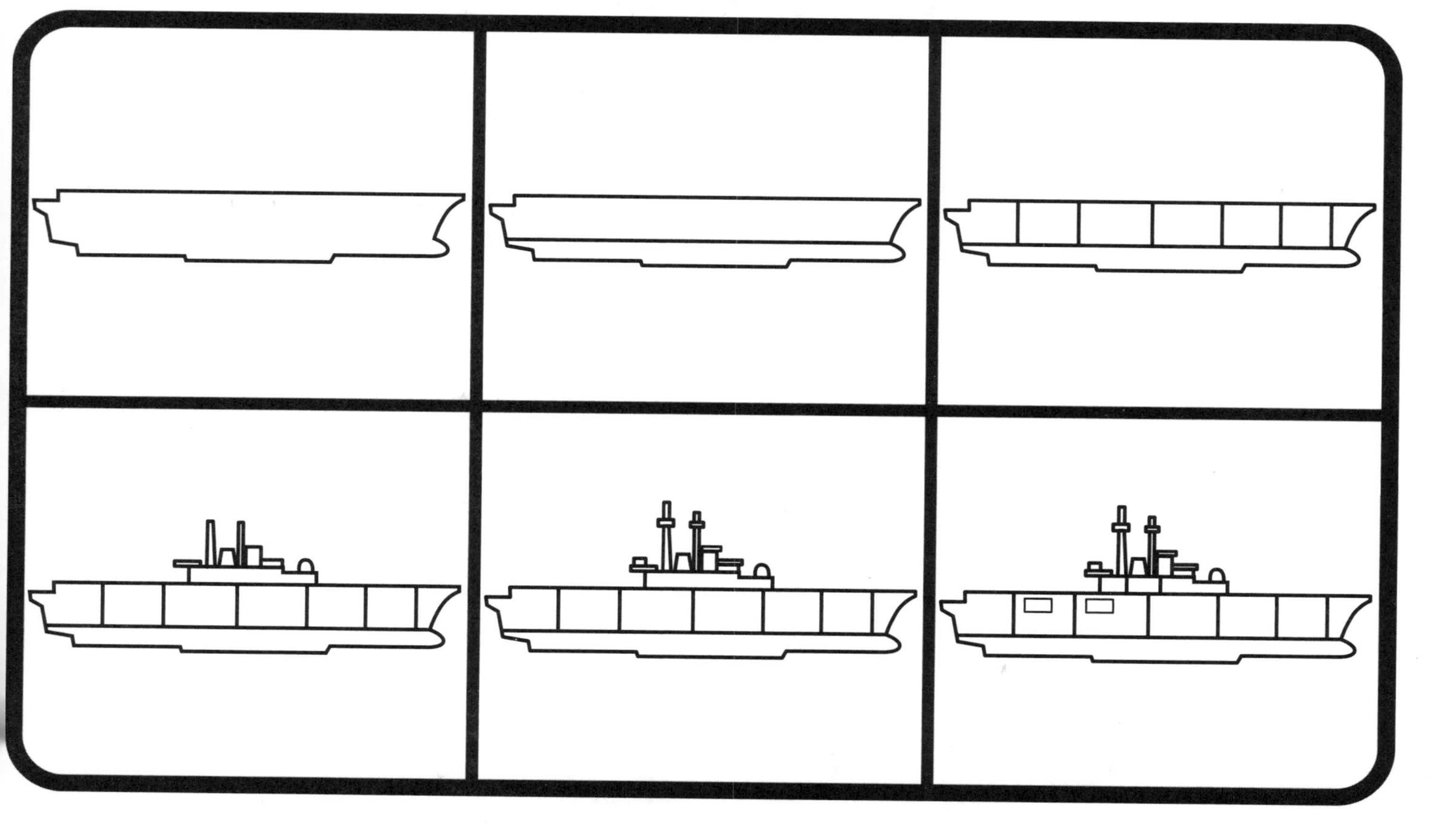

USS KITTY HAWK

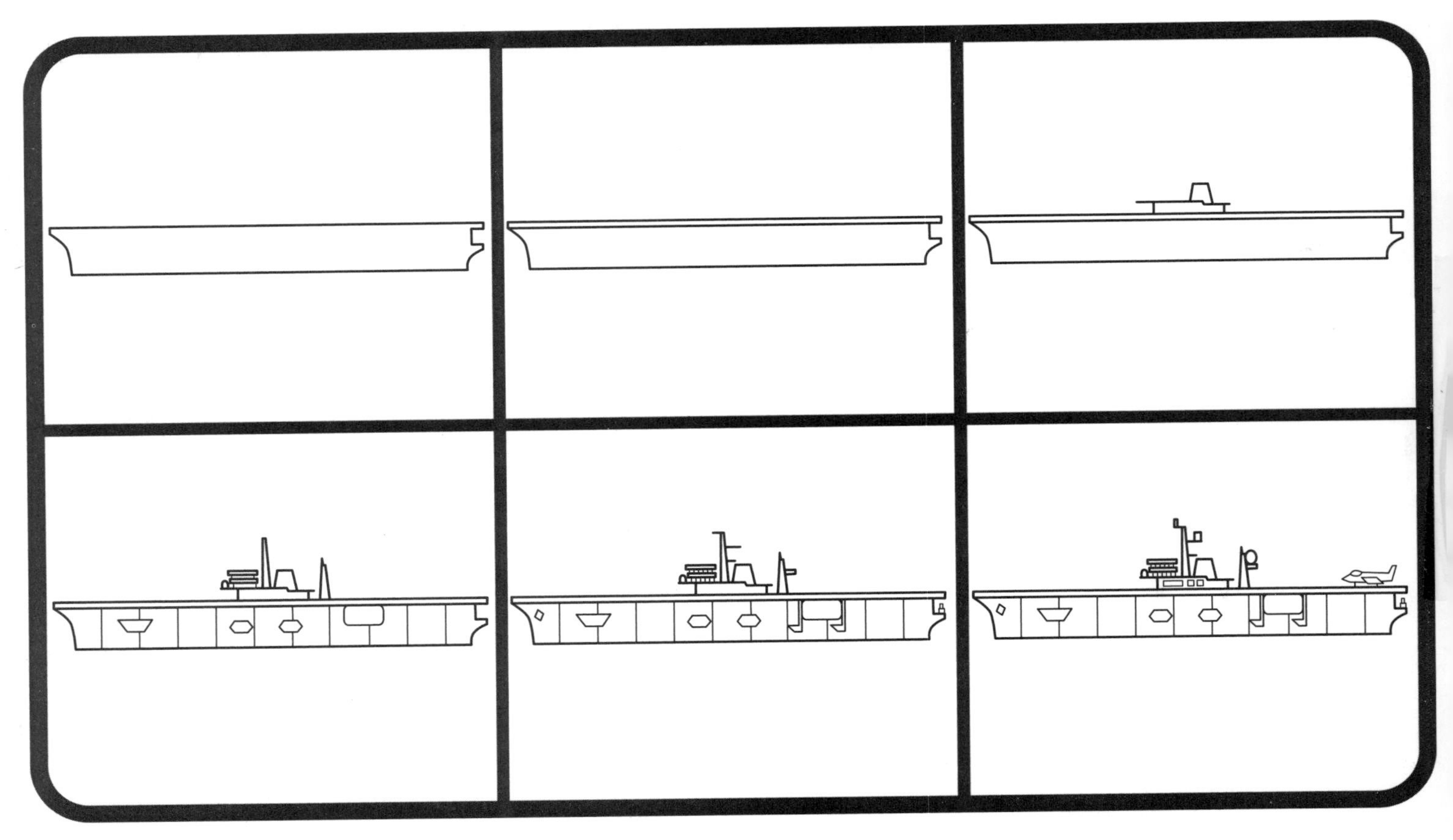

USS INDEPENDENCE

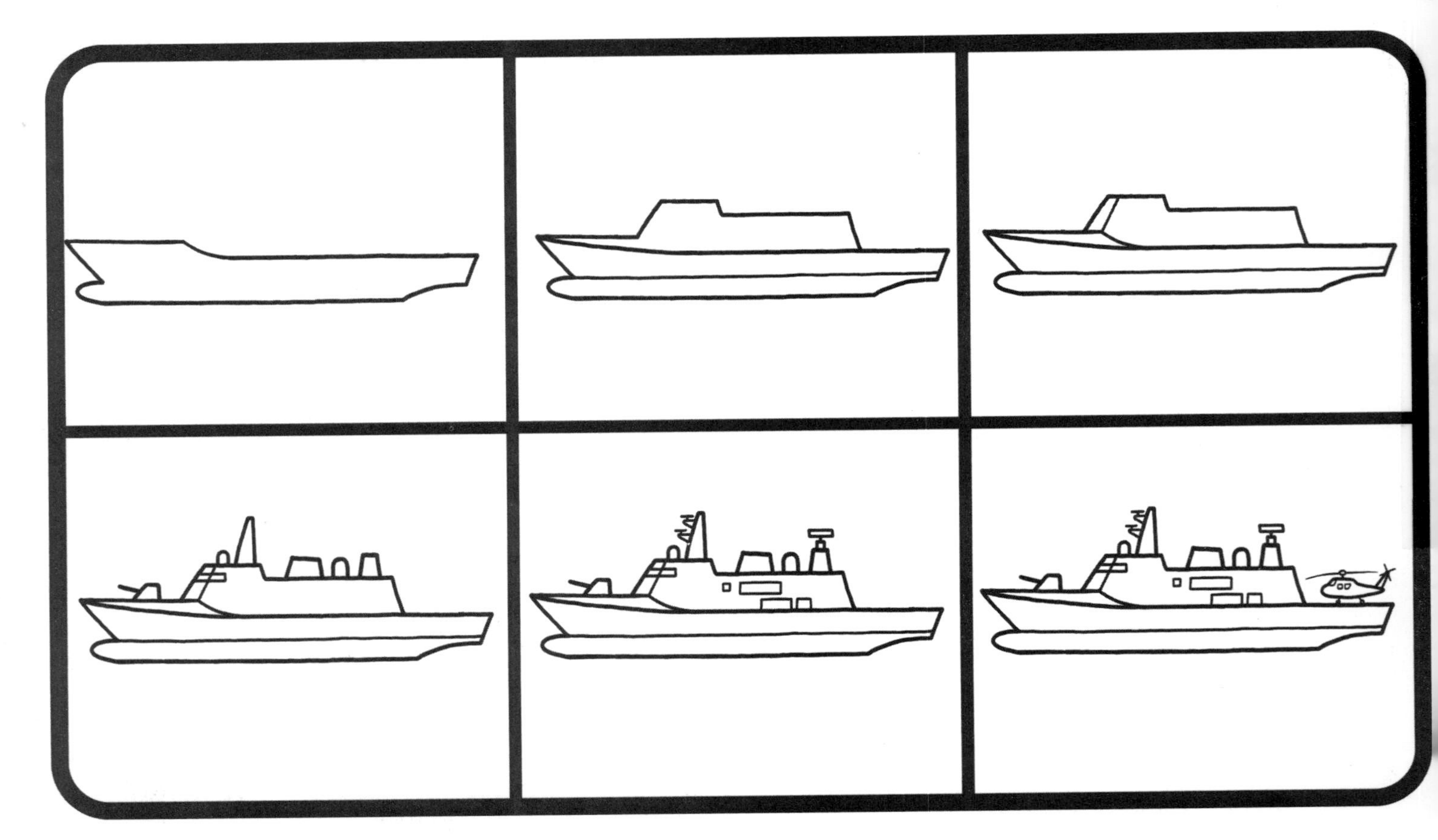

SCHNEIDER CA1

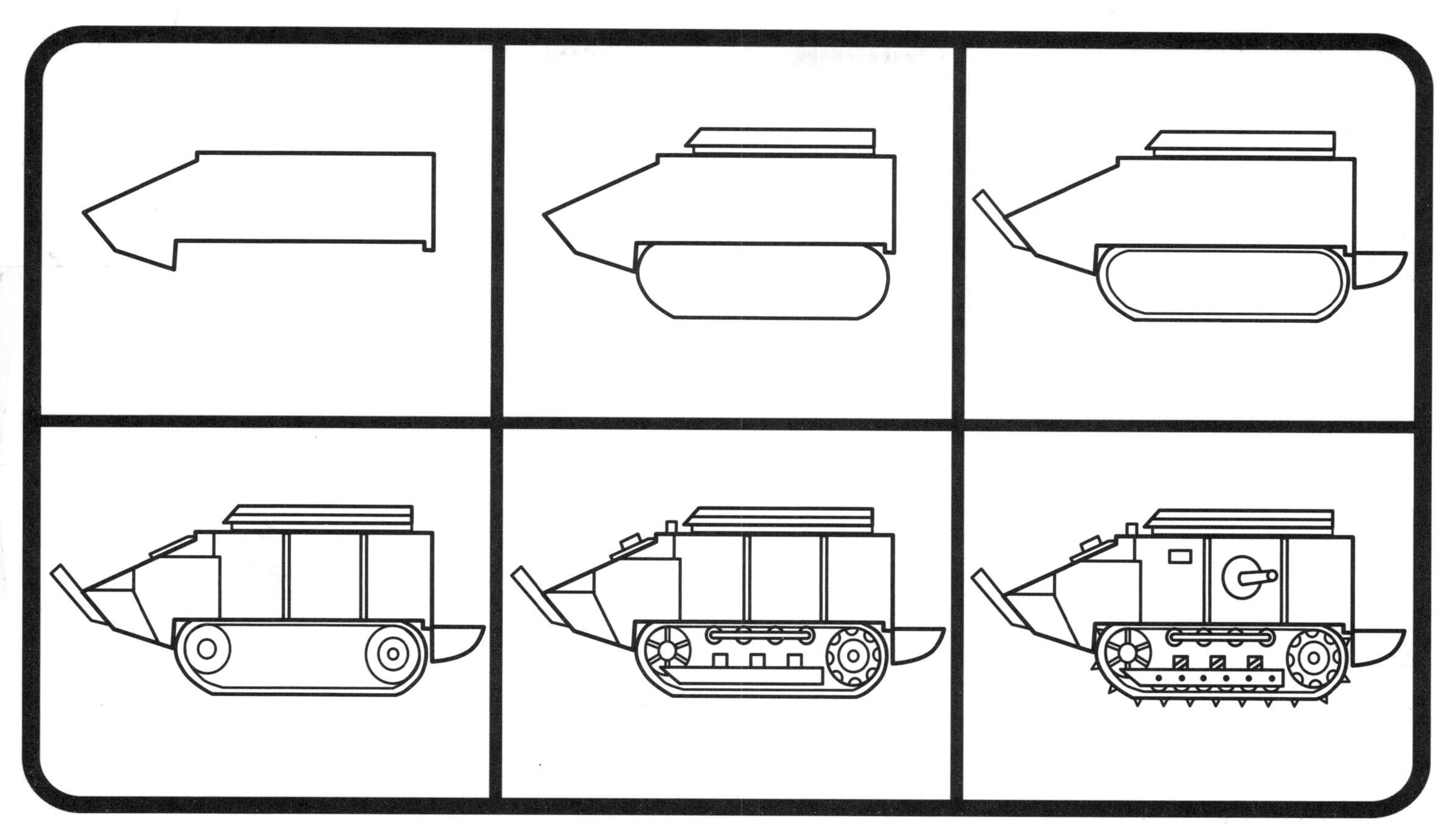

VICKERS MBT TANK

BLACKHAWK HELICOPTER

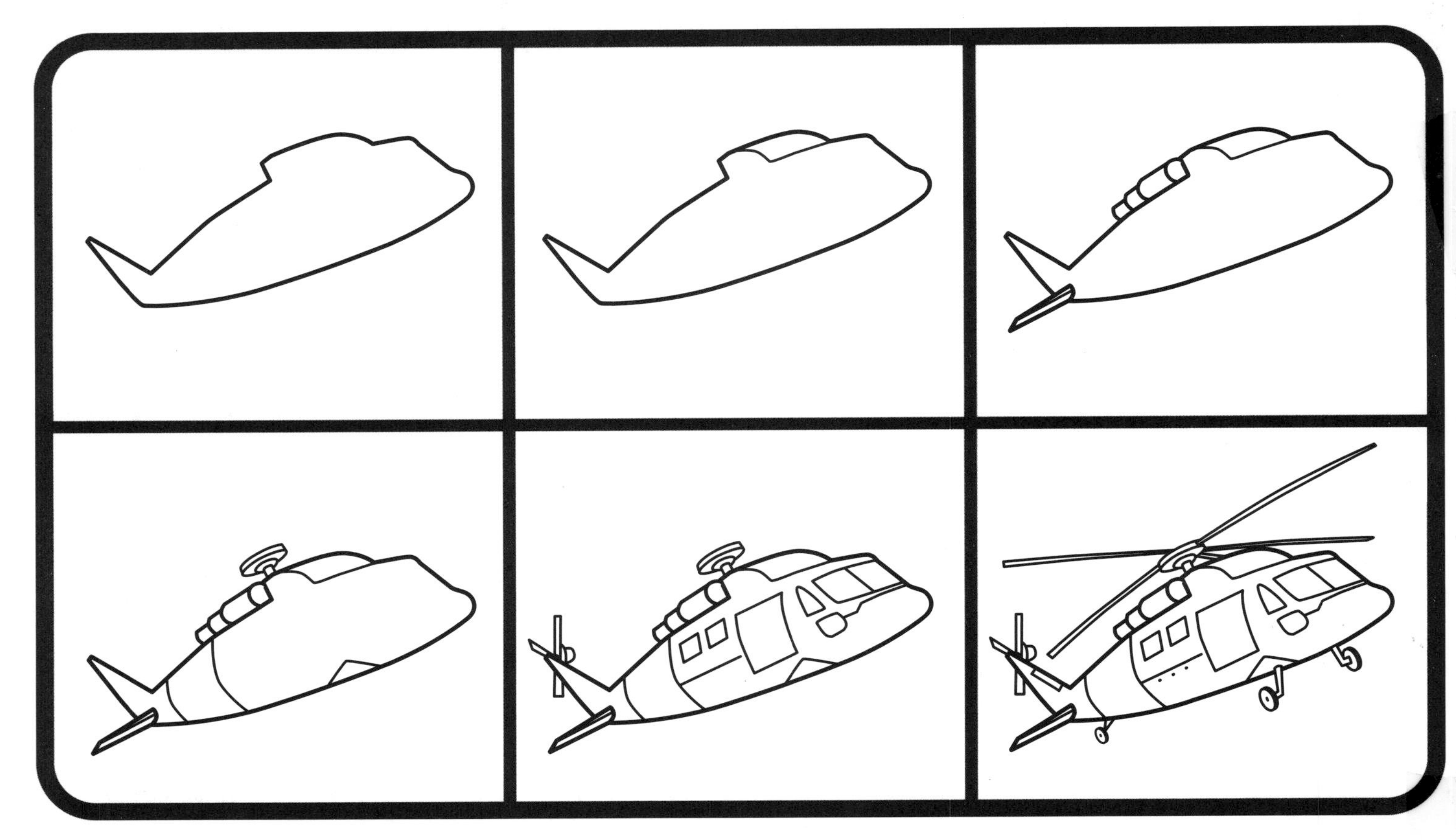

CHINOOK HELICOPTER

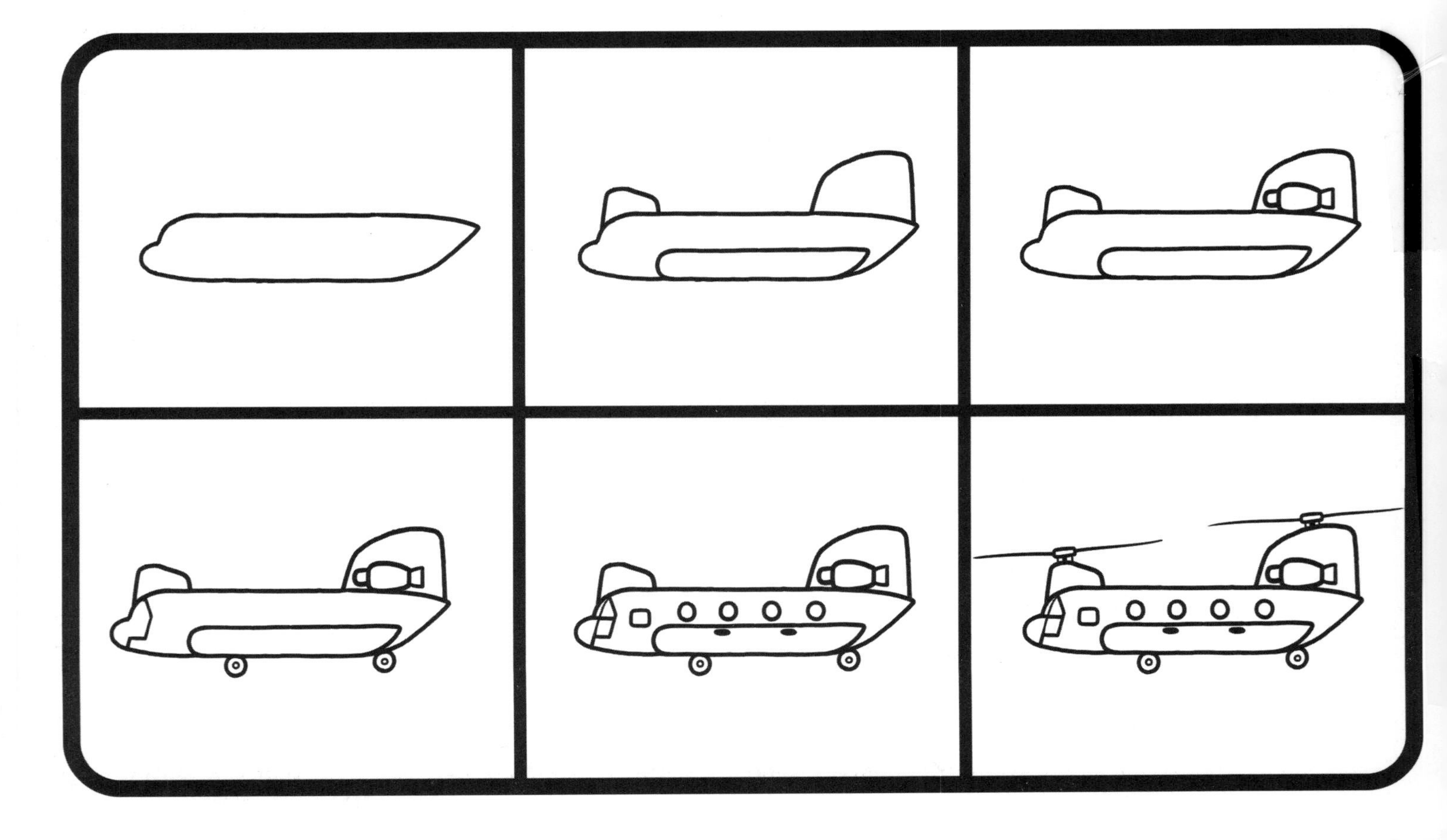

F-16 FIGHTING FALCON

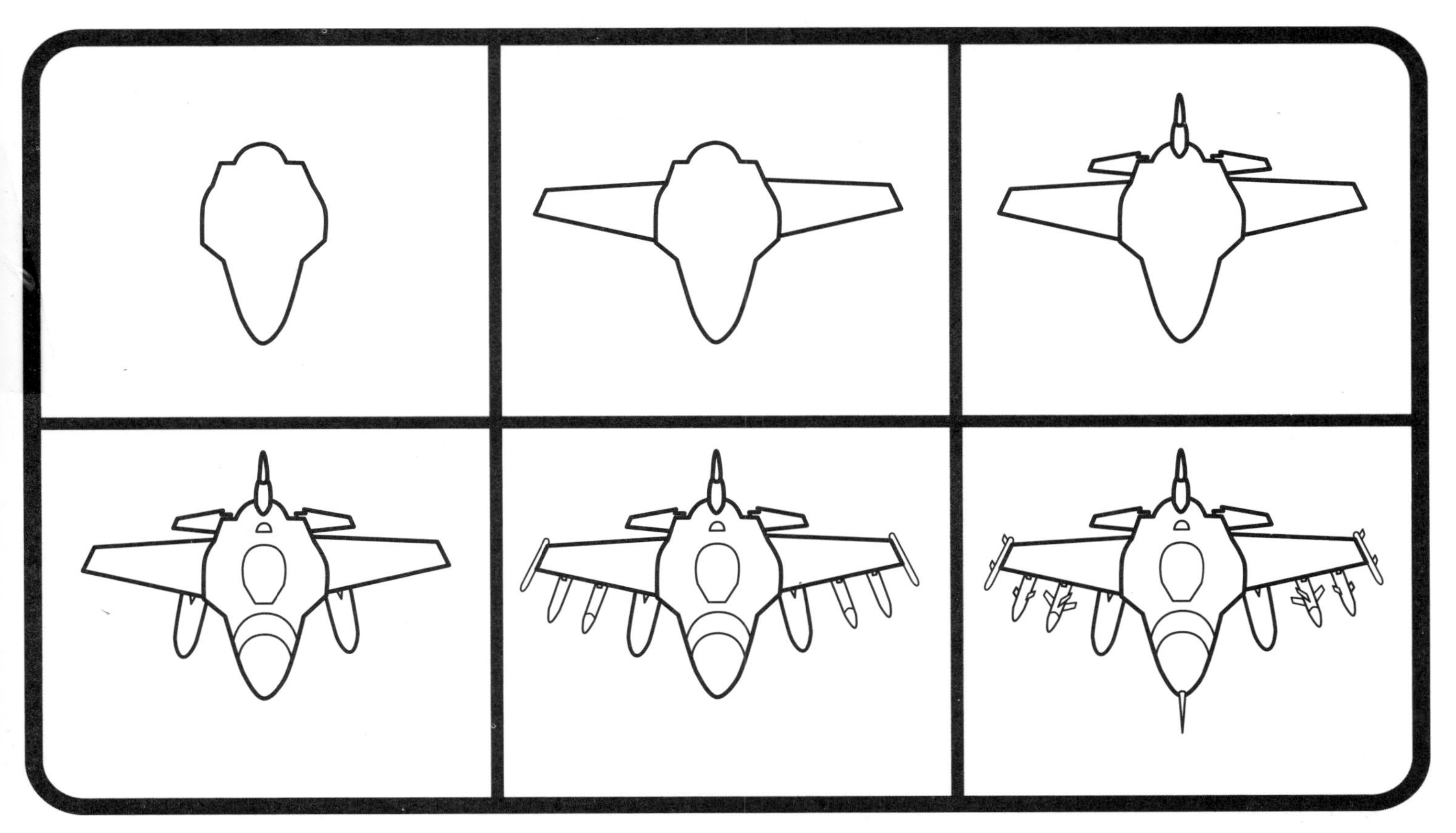

EUROFIGHTER TYPHOON

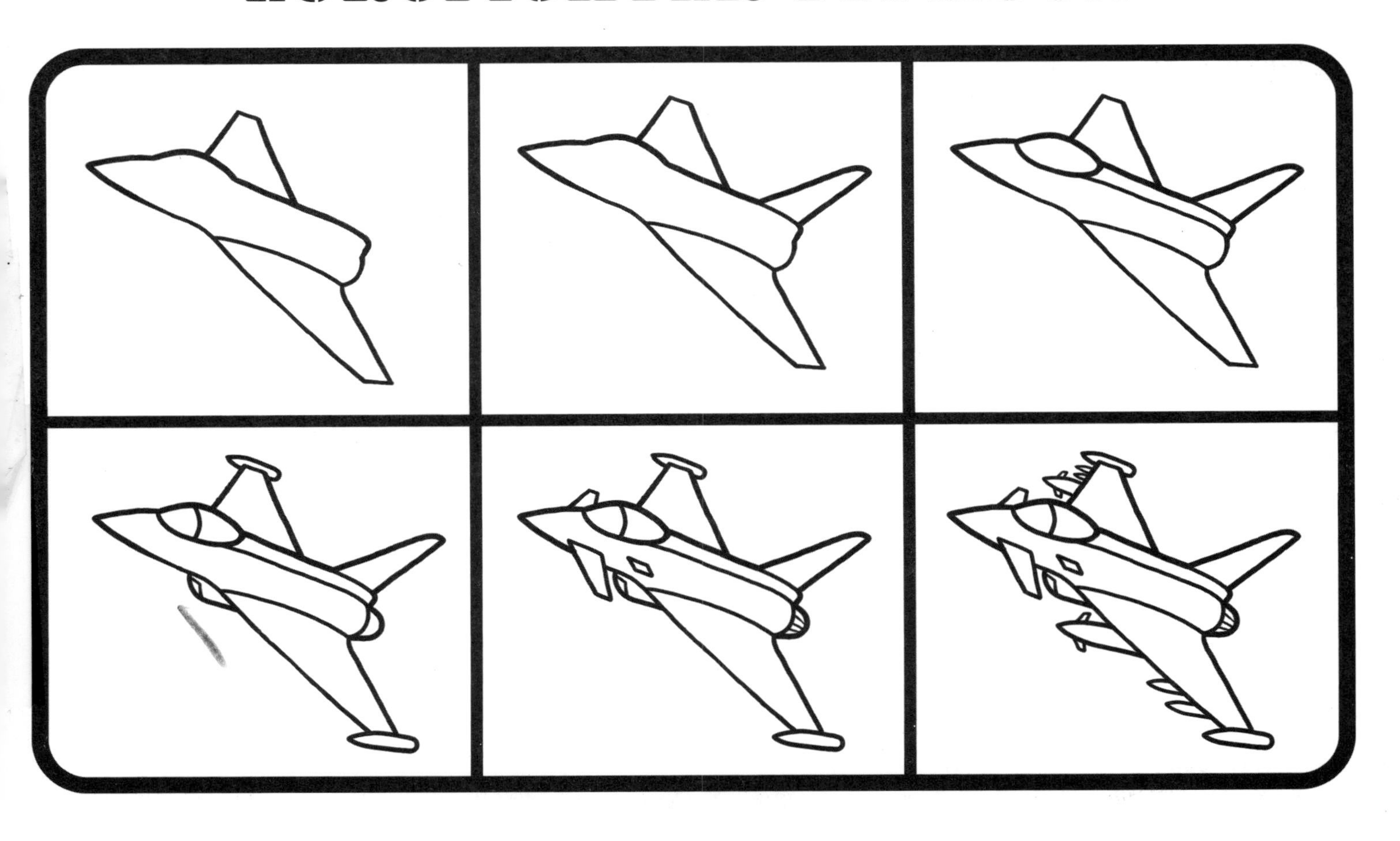

M103 HEAVY TANK

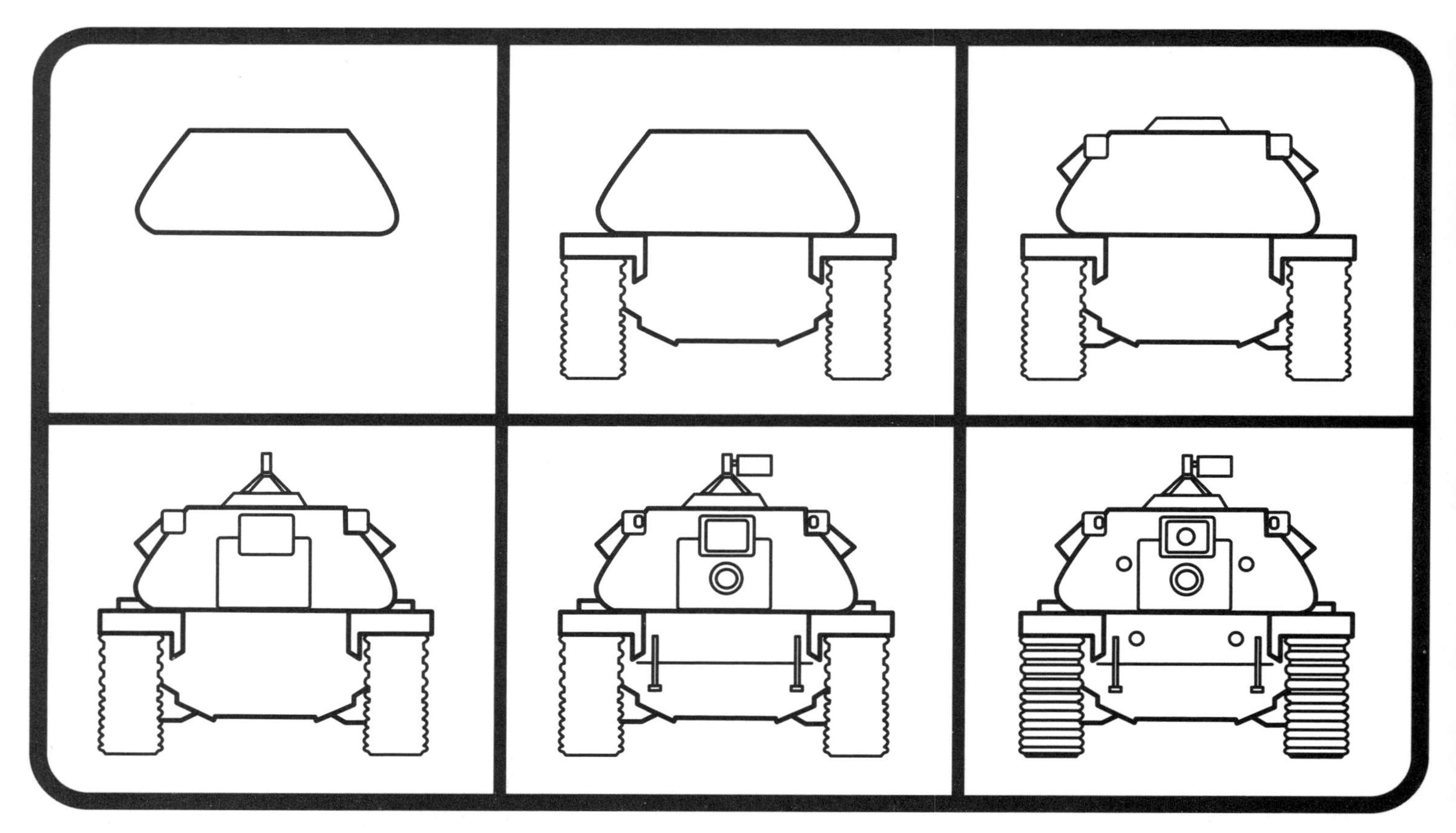

ARMORED FLAMETHROWER

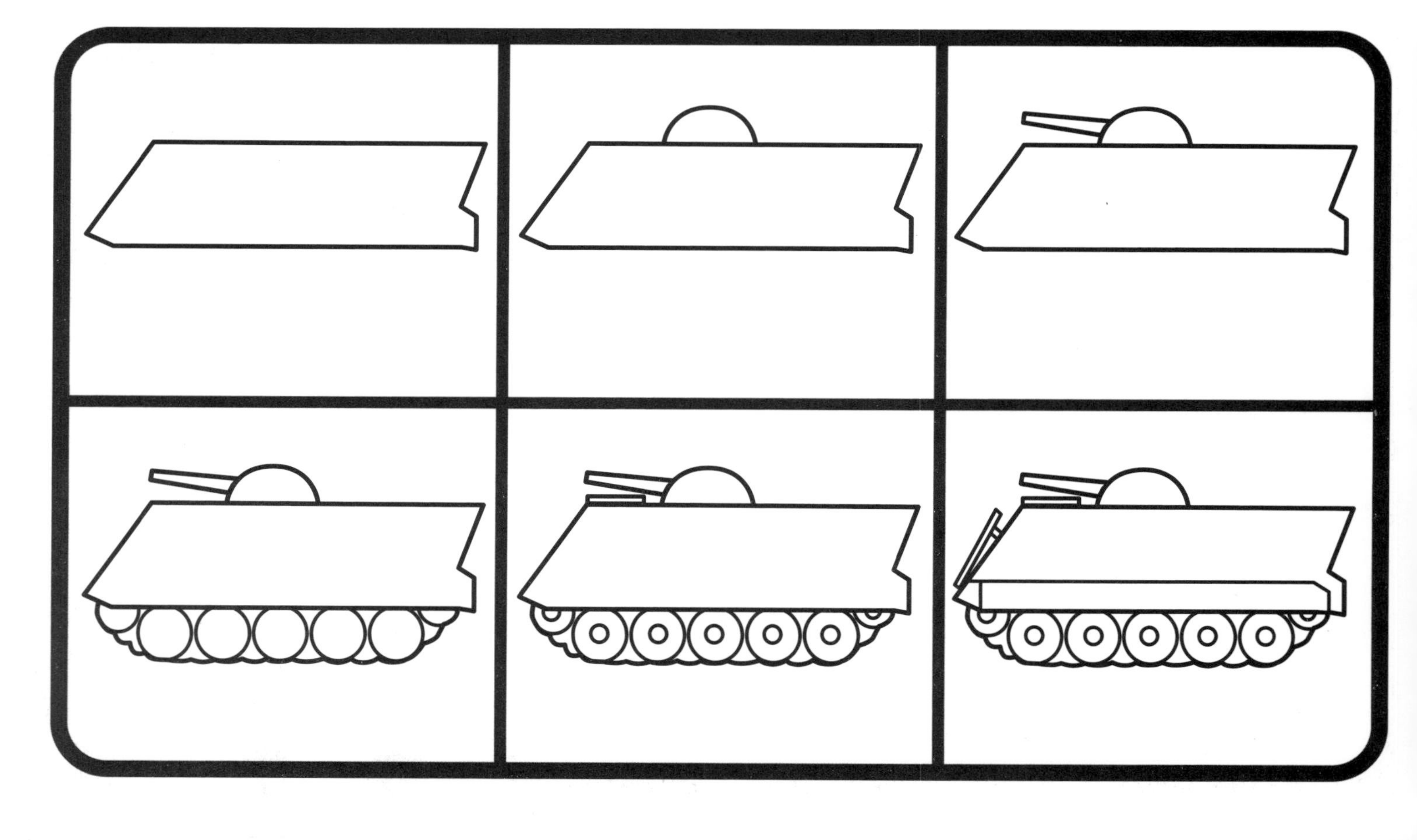

LOCKHEED MARTIN F-35 LIGHTNING

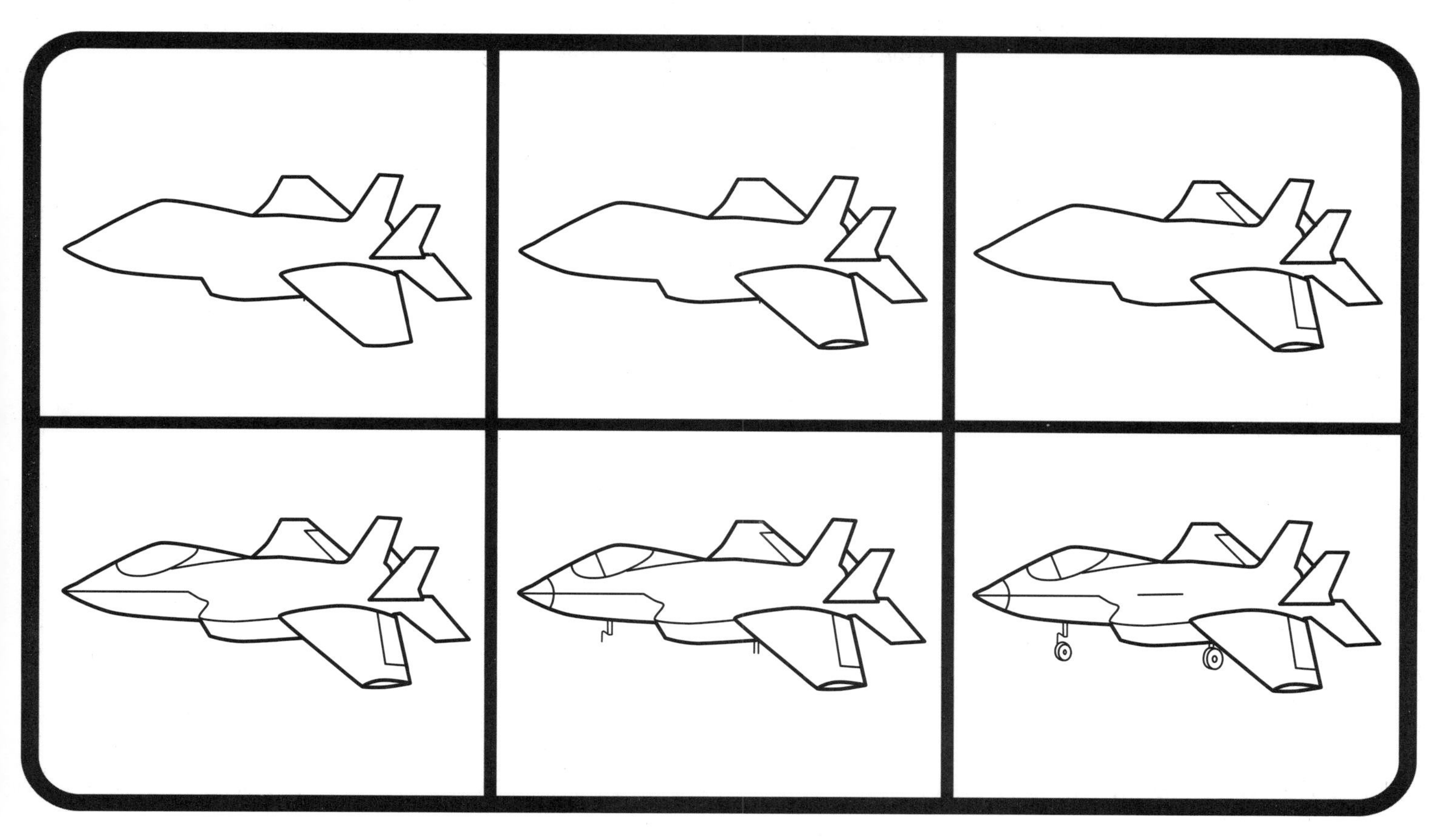

HARRIER JUMP JET

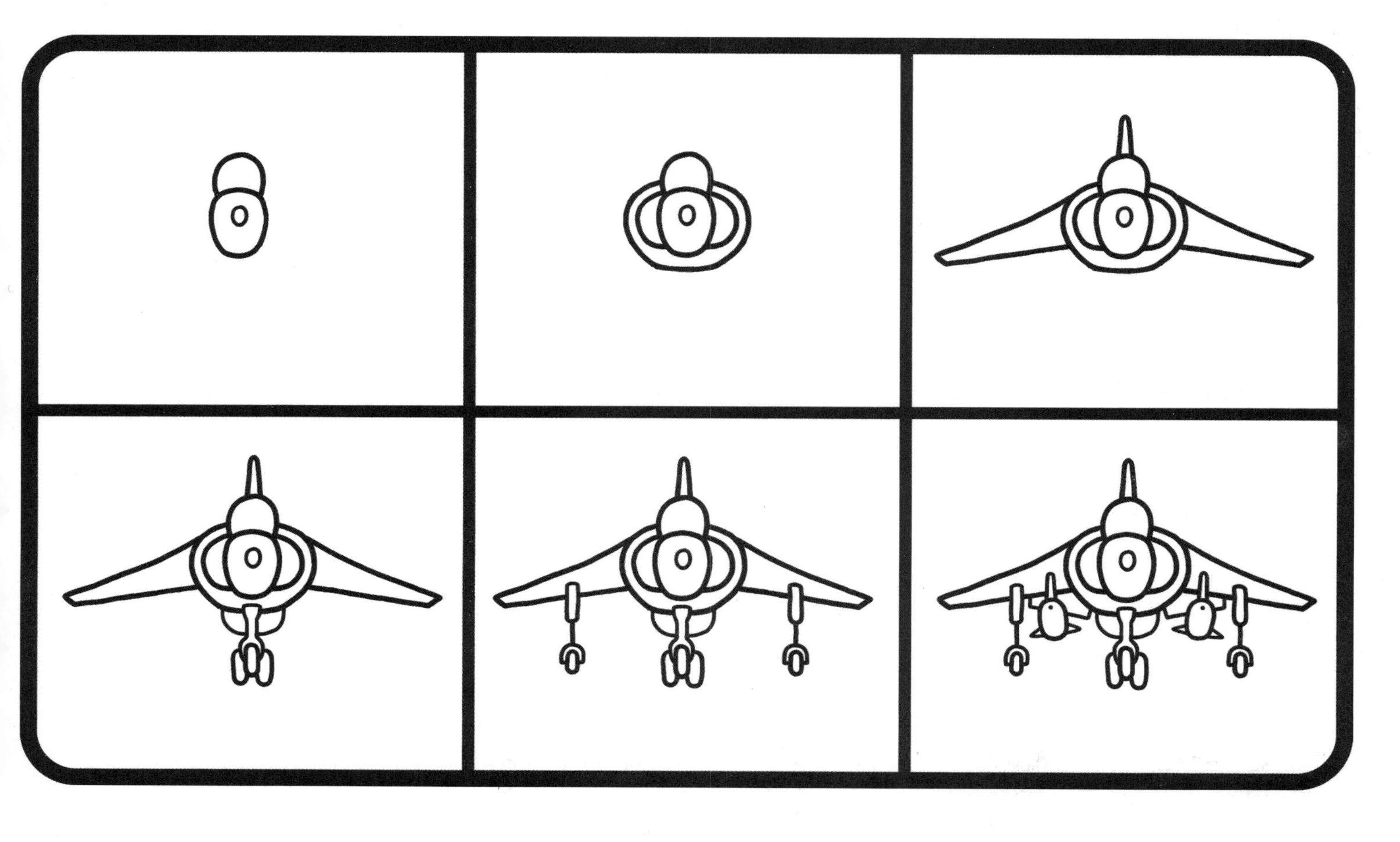

CH-21C HELICOPTER

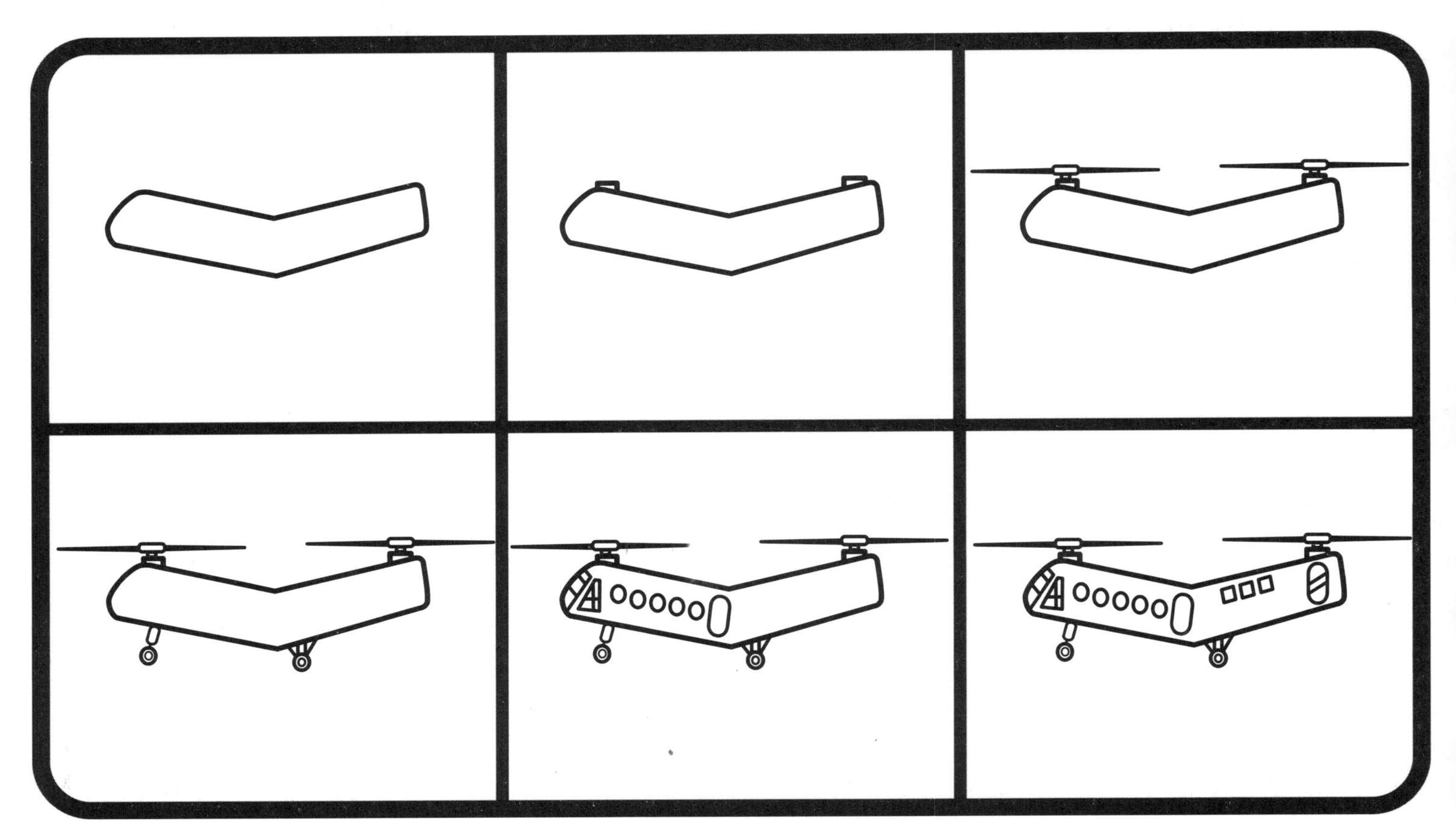

GAZELLE HELICOPTER

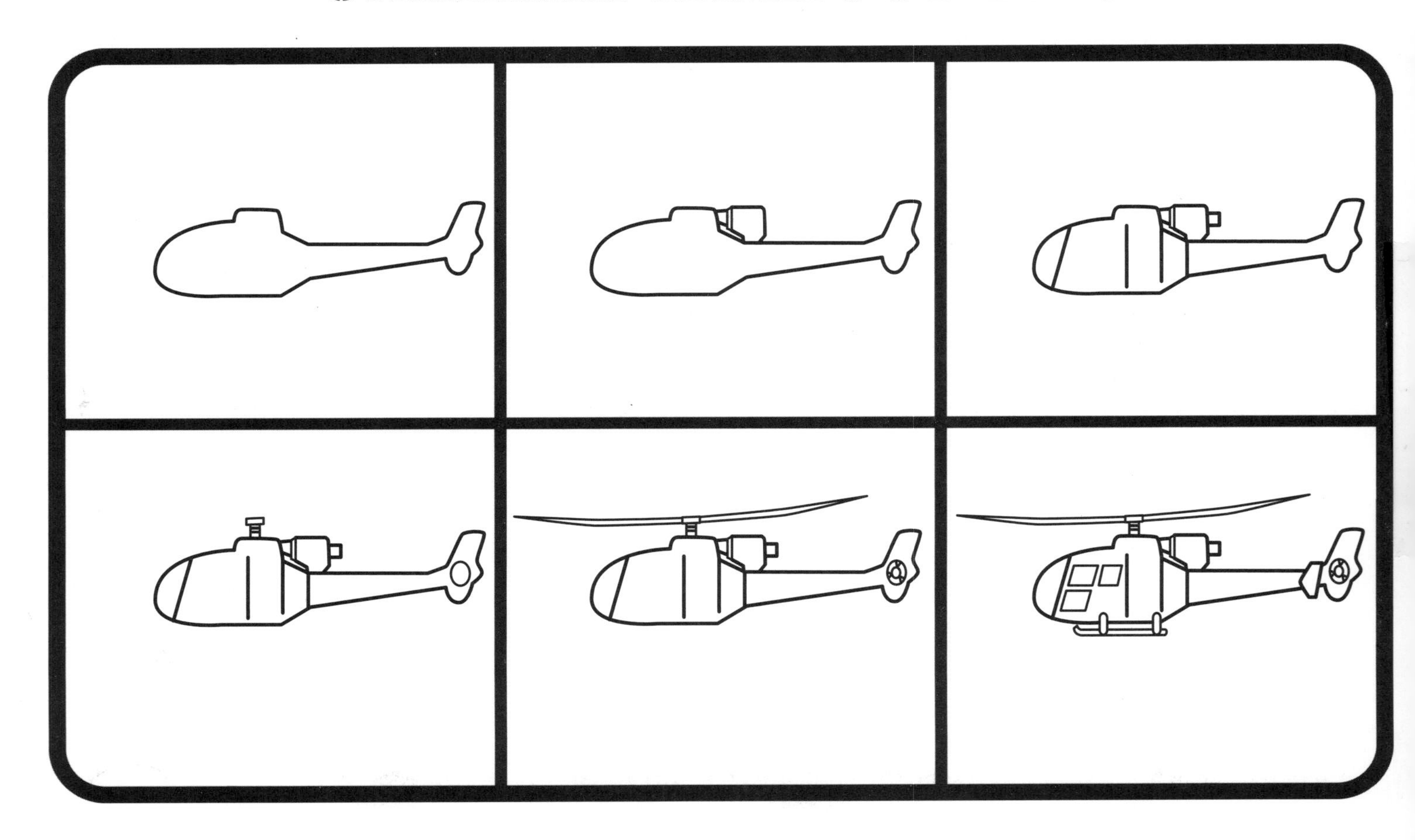

M1A2 TUSK TANK

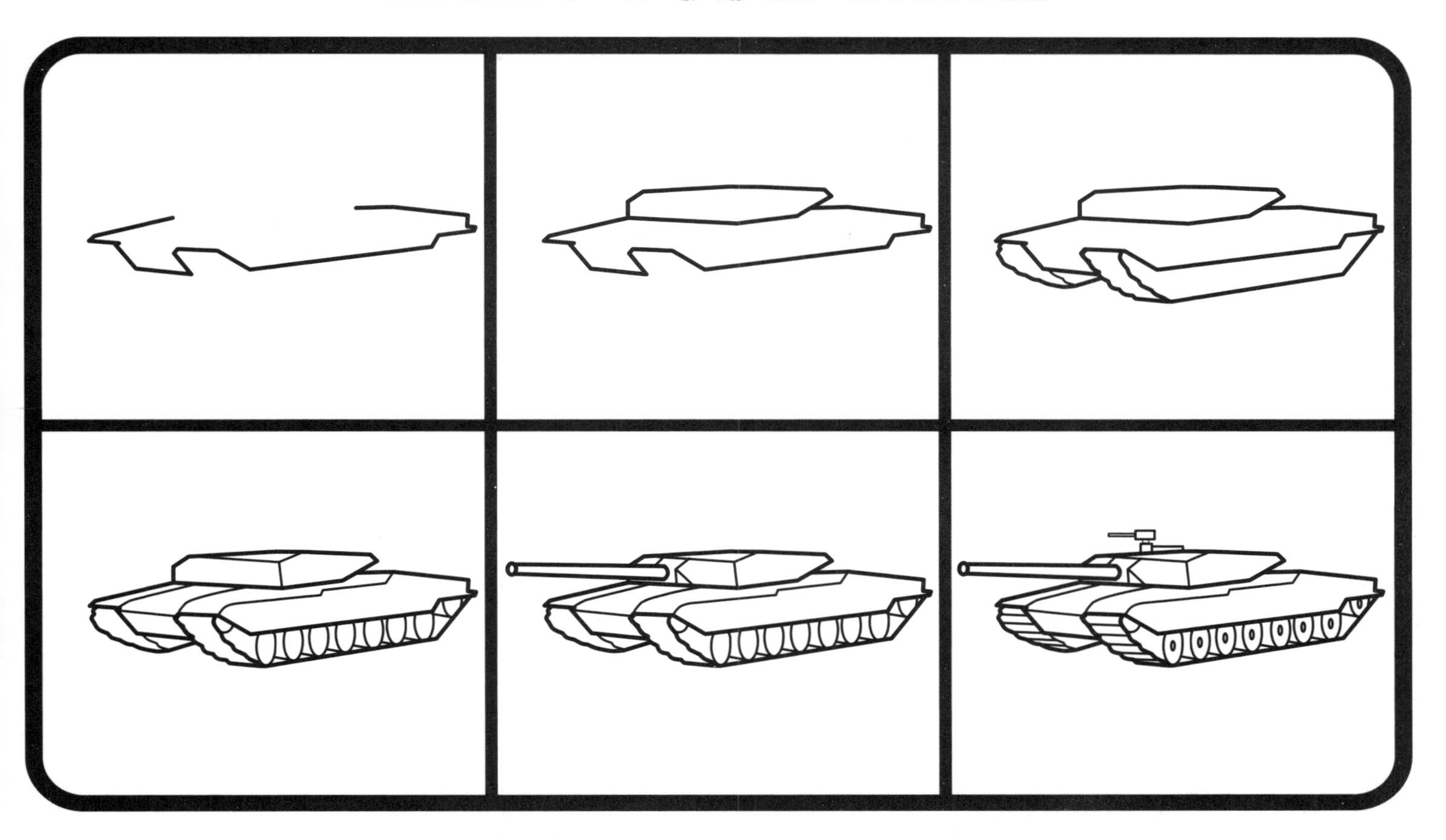

RENAULT FT TANK

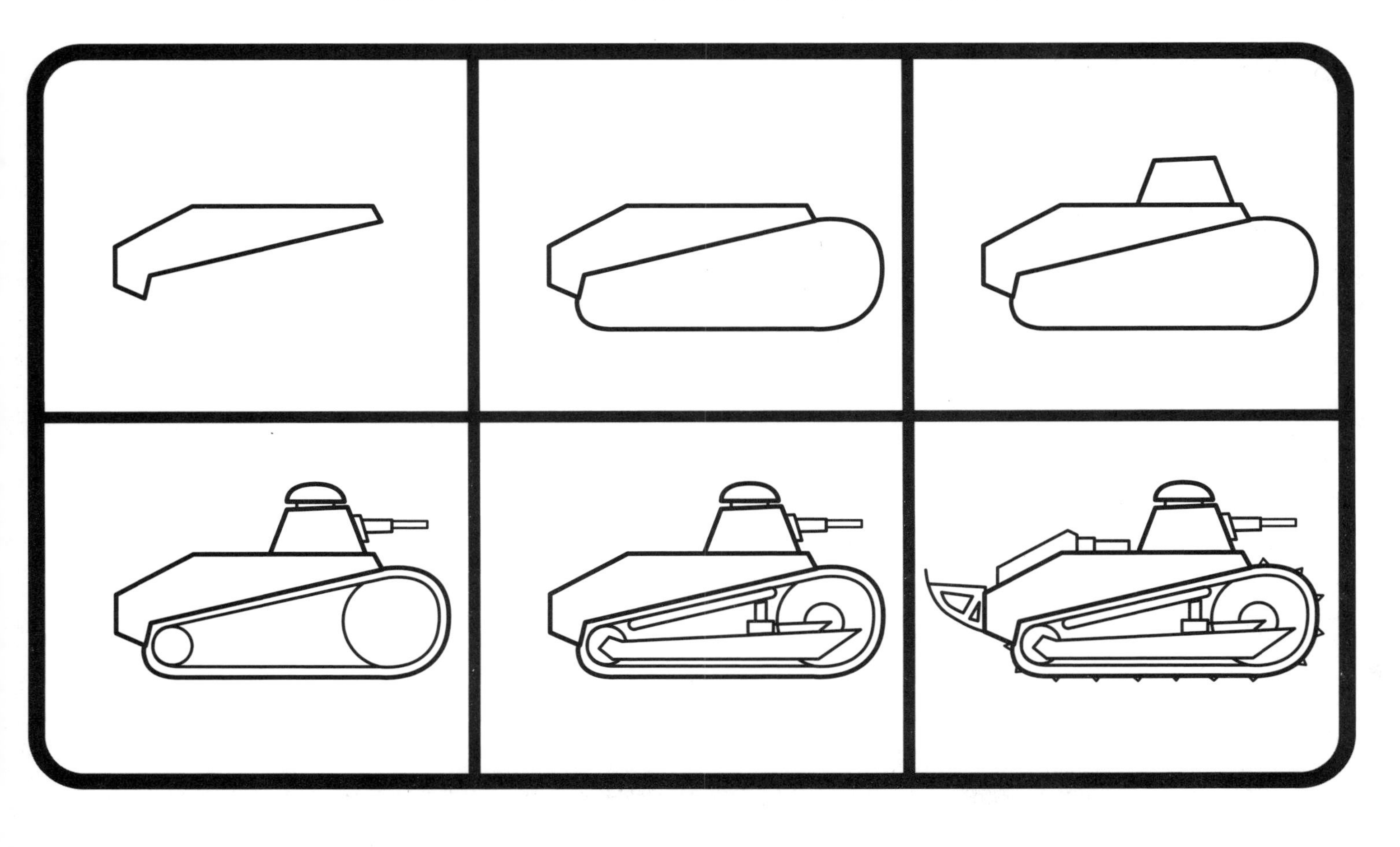

FV603 PERSONNEL CARRIER

M113 ARMORED PERSONNEL CARRIER

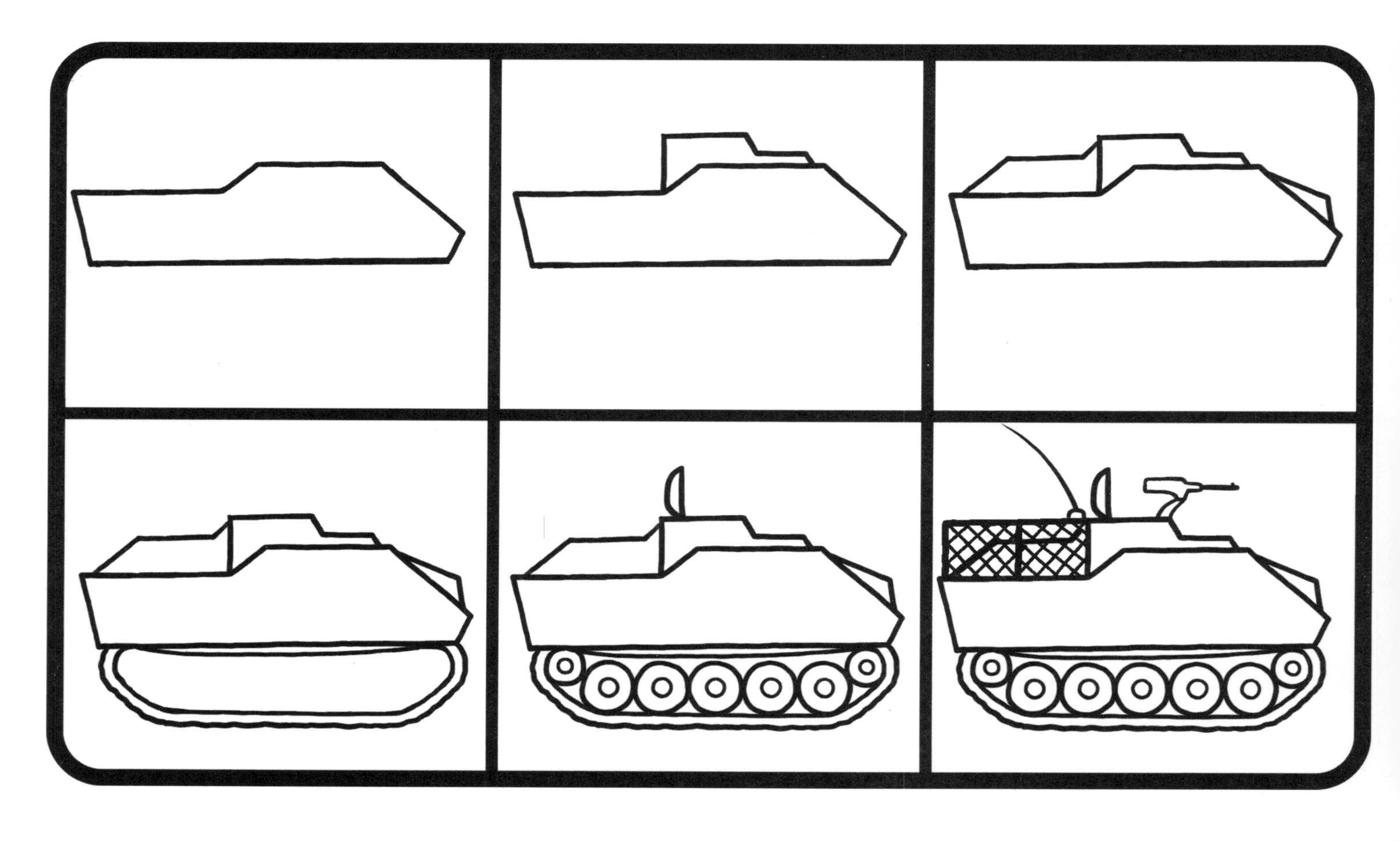

P-47 THUNDERBOLT

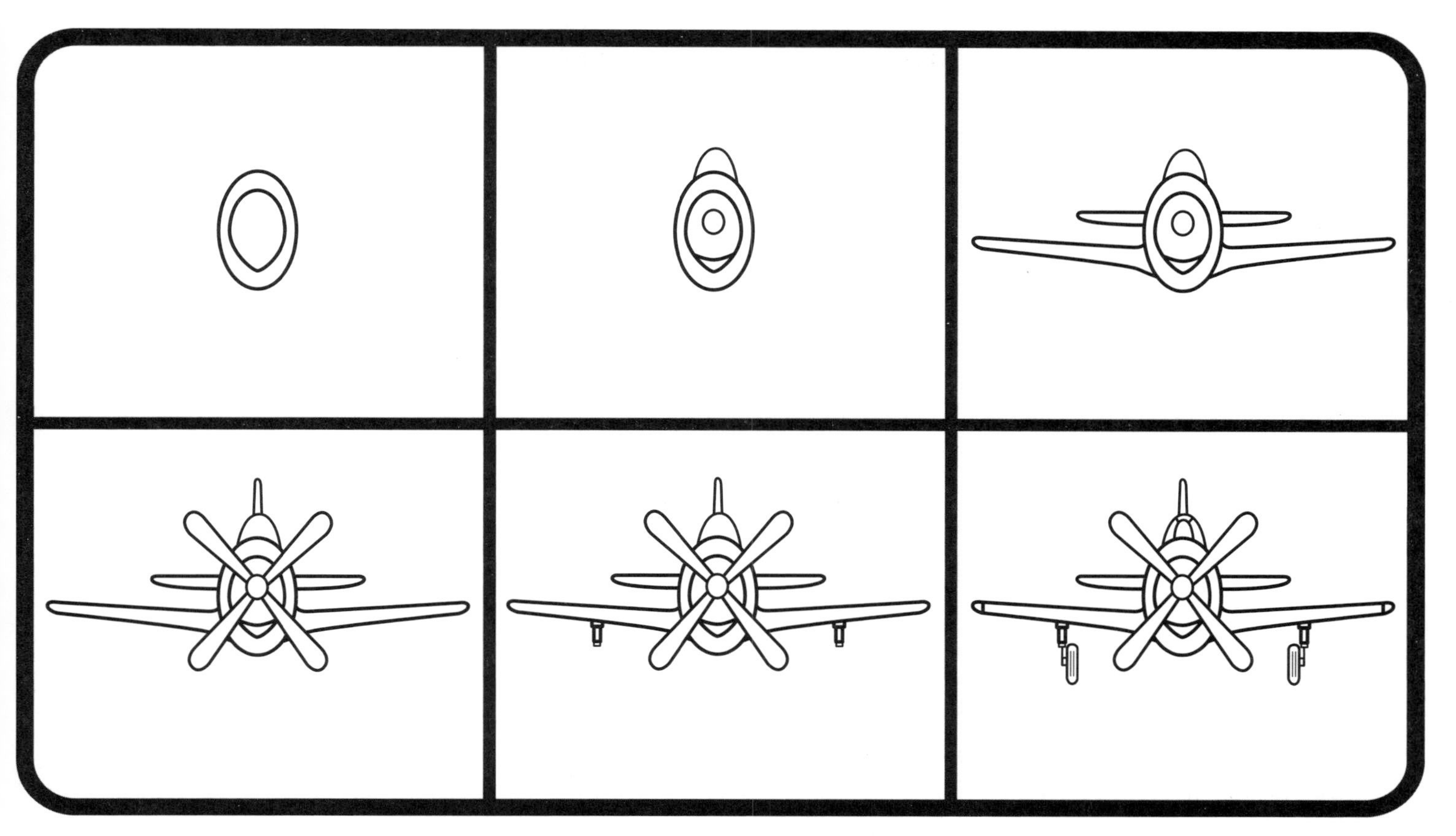

HAWKER HURRICANE

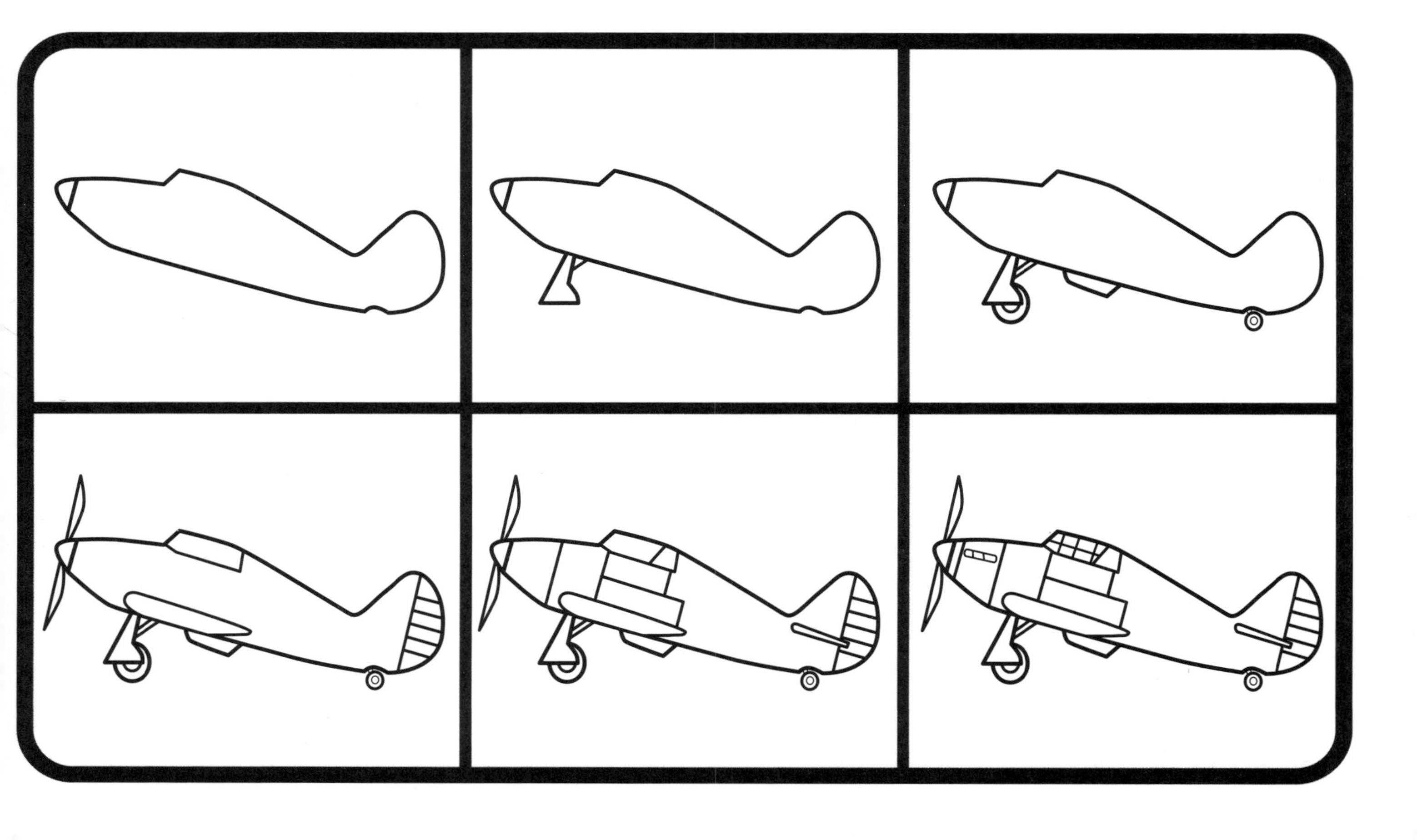

VICKERS F.B.5 GUNBUS

FOKKER EINDECKER

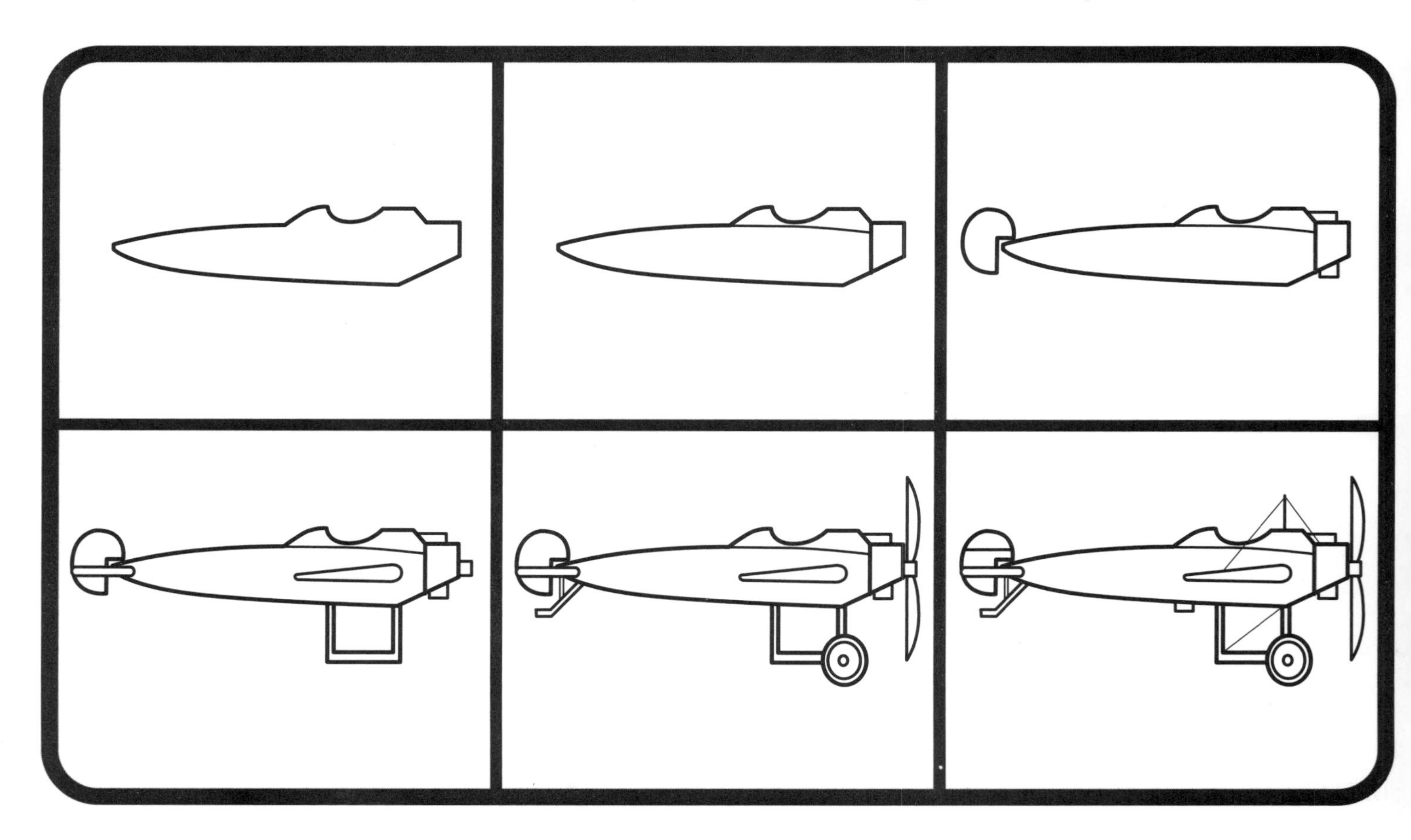

SUPERMARINE SPITFIRE

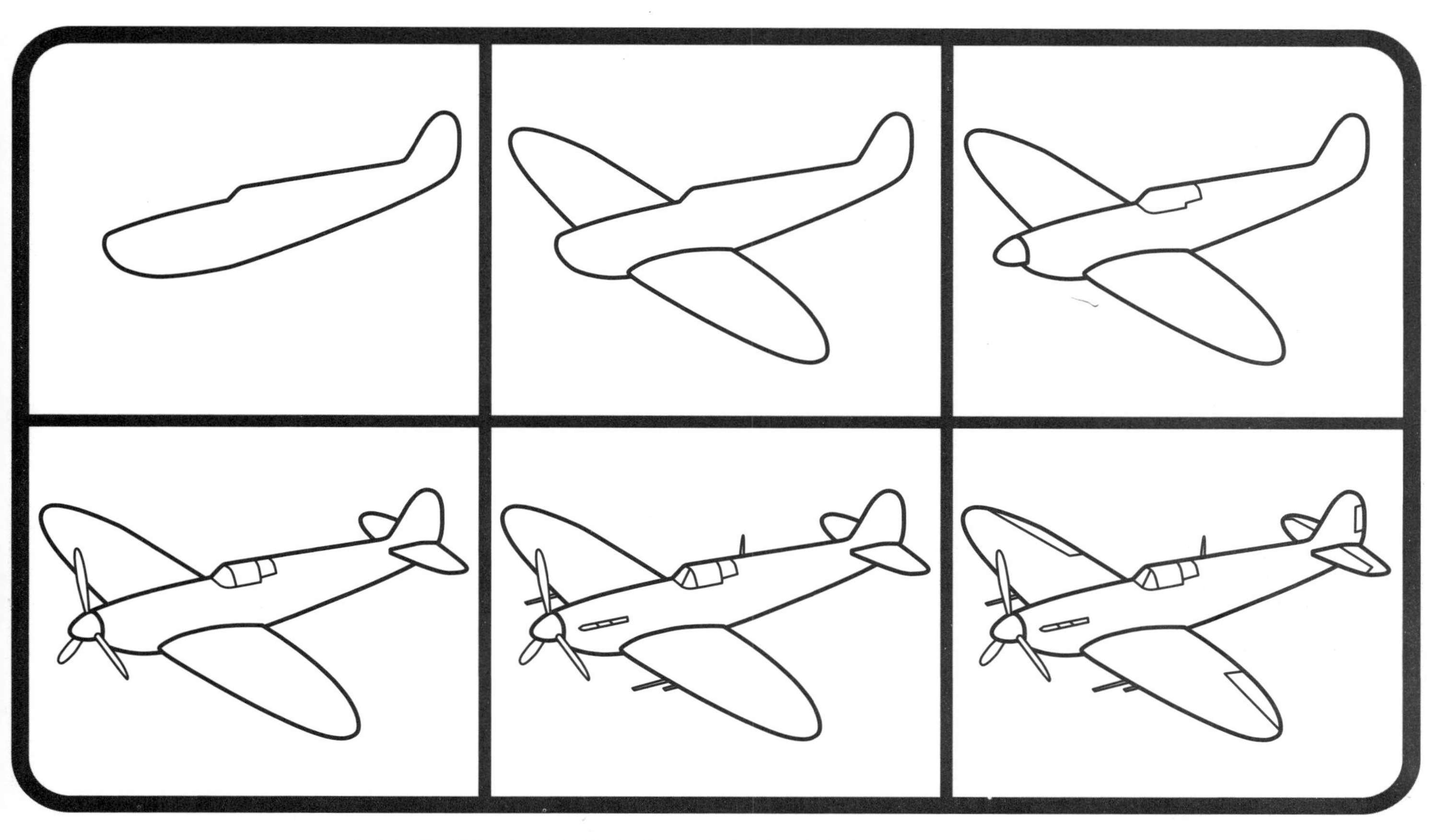

FOKKER TRIPLANE

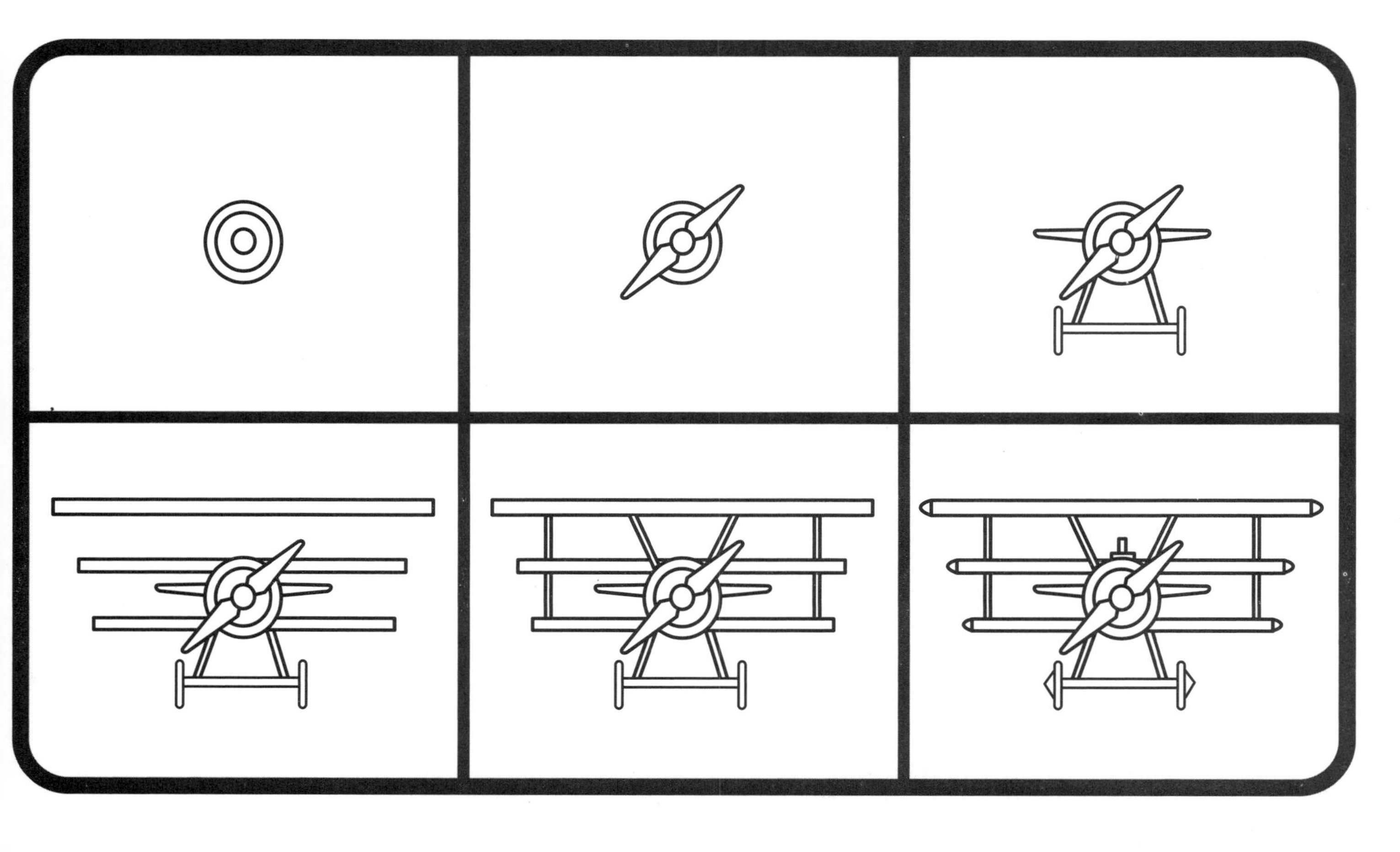

LOCKHEED HC-130

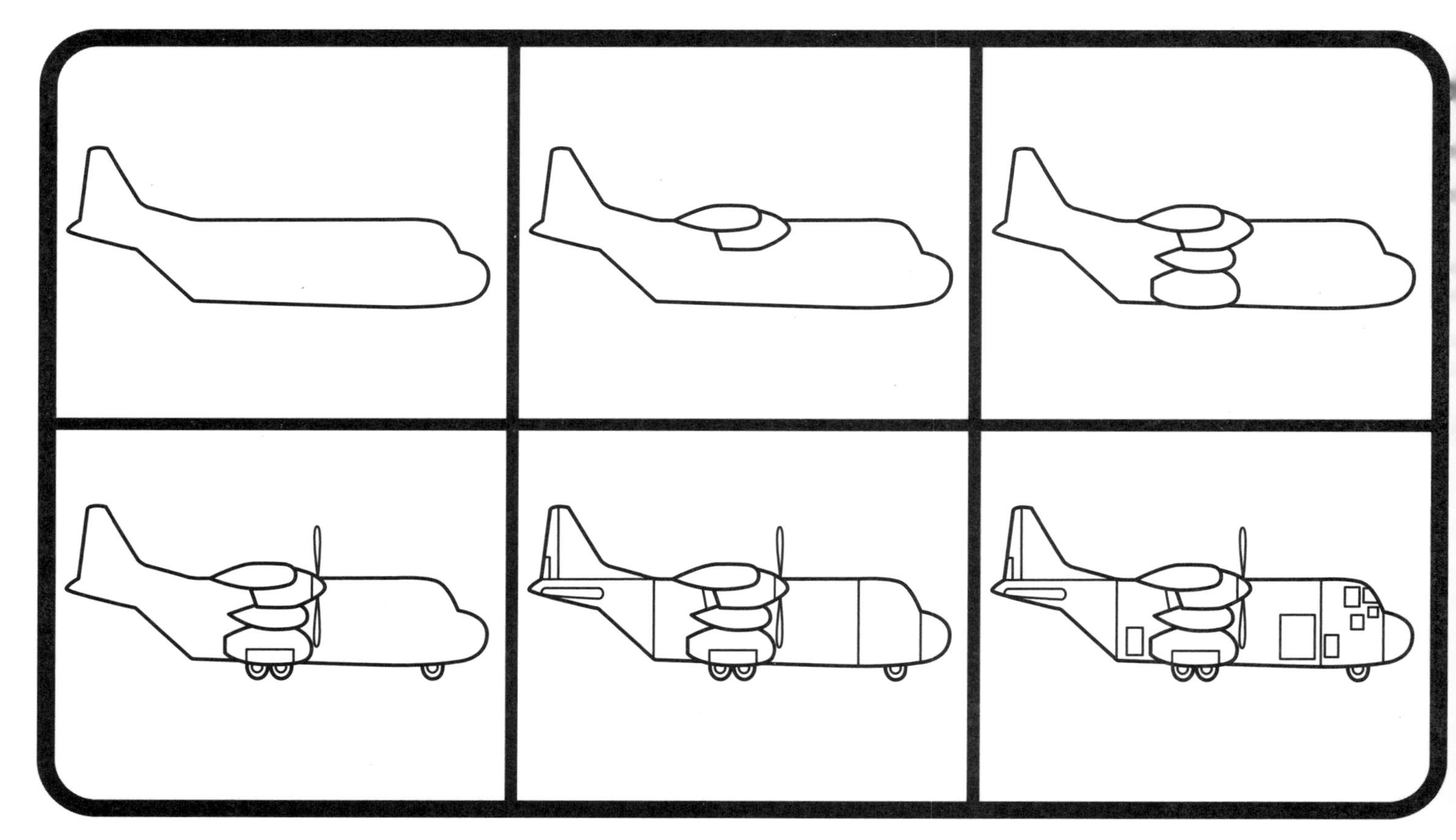

STEALTH FIGHTER

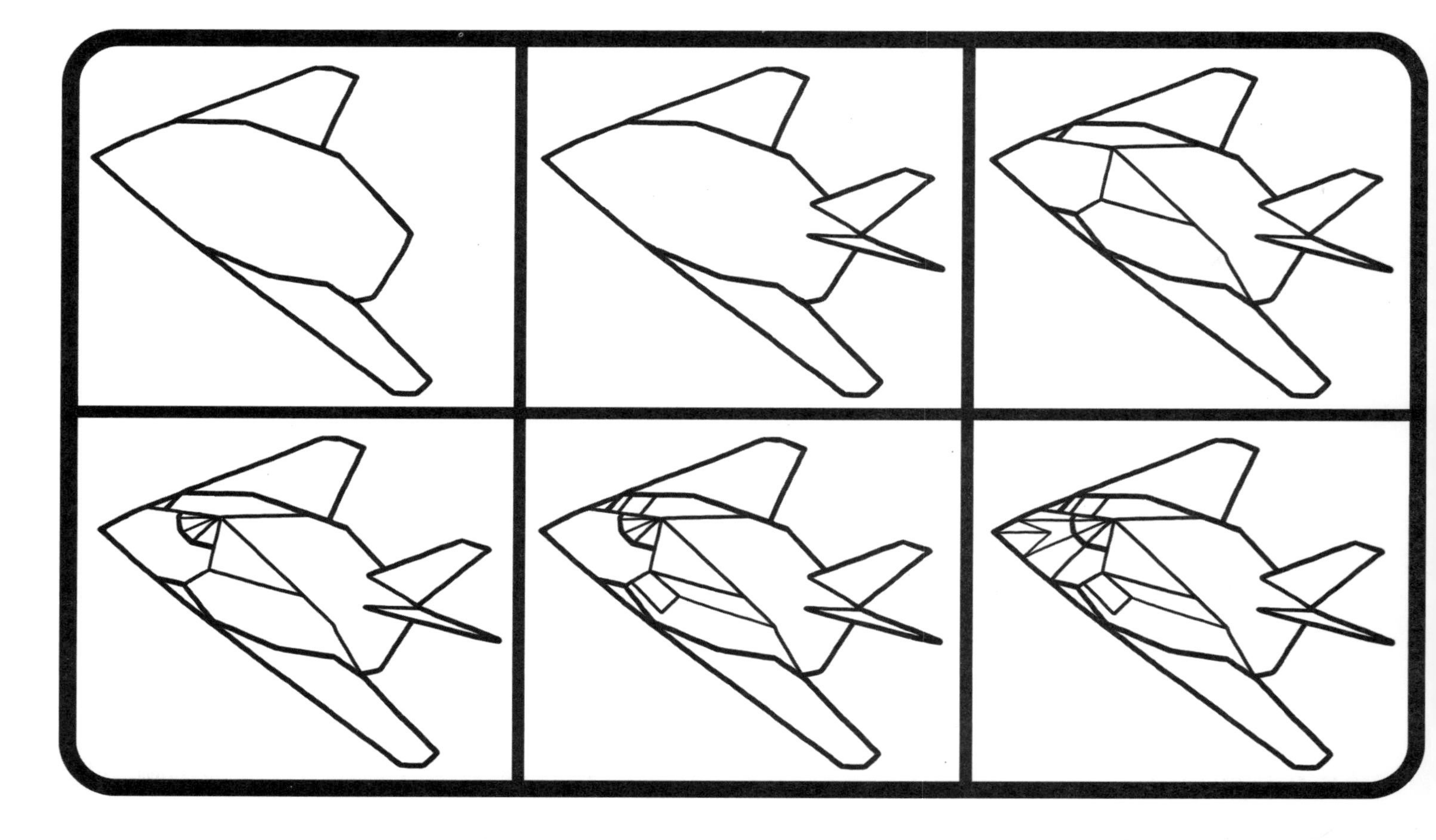

USS ANNAPOLIS SUBMARINE

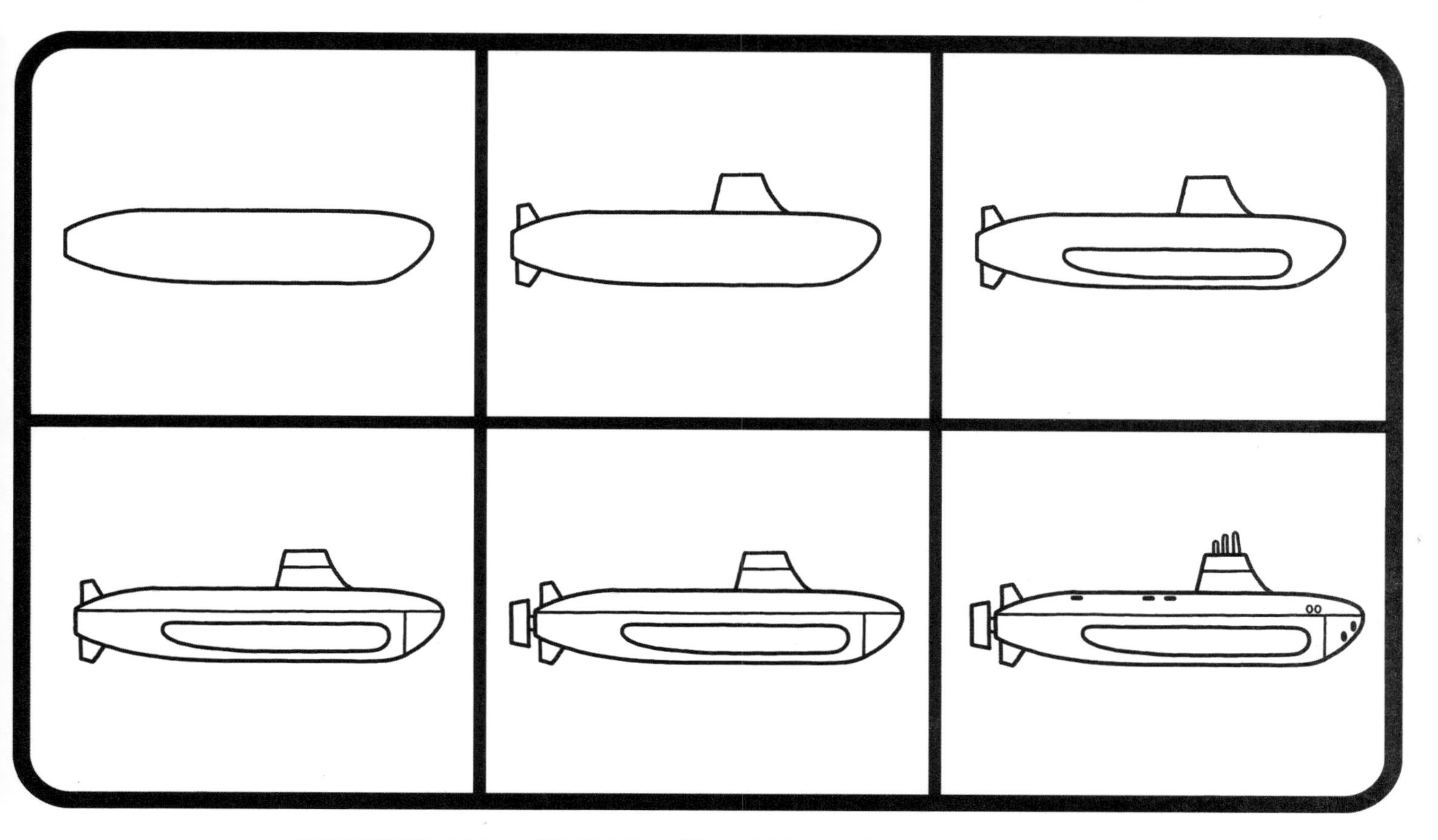

TYPE XXI SUBMARINE

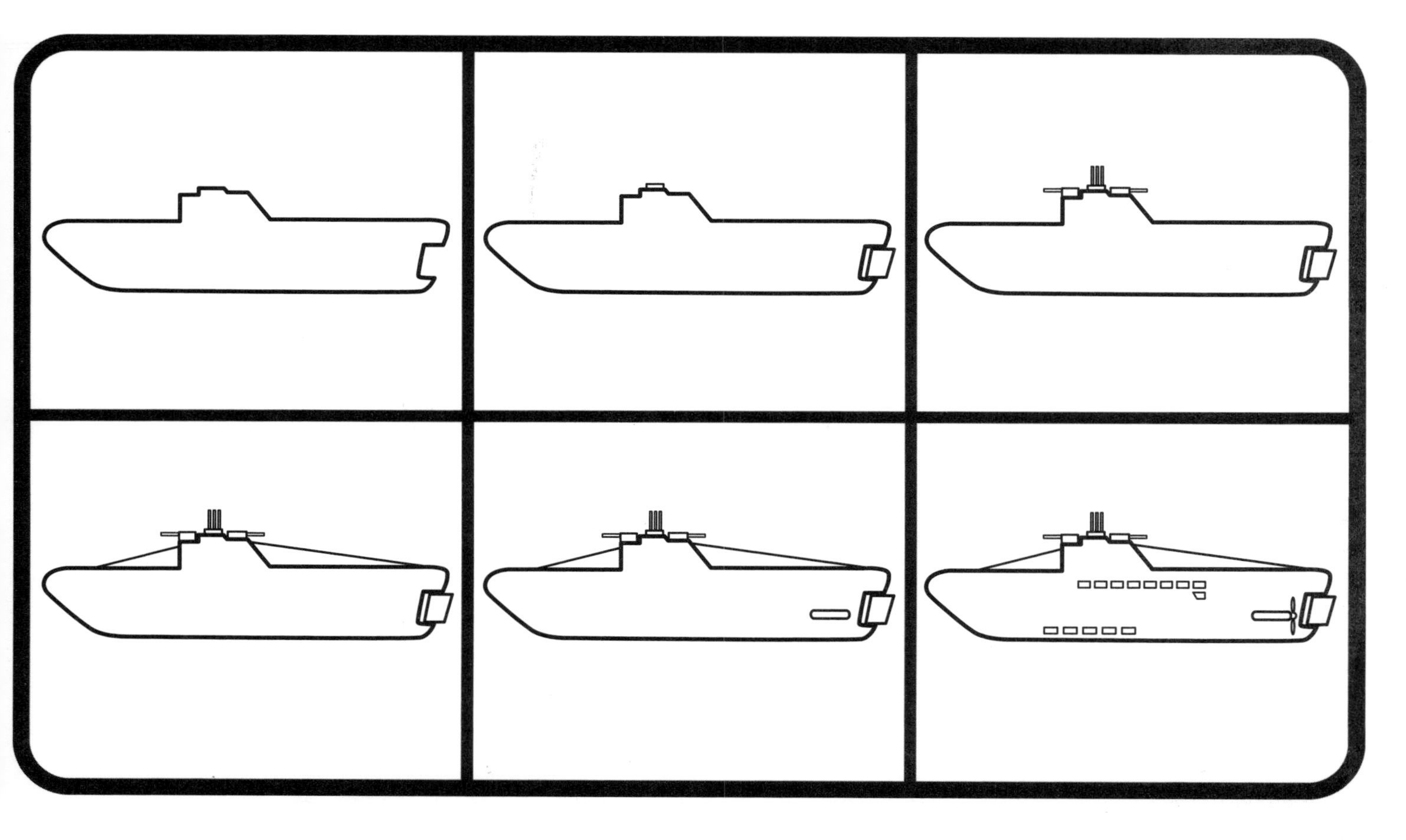

NORTON 16H

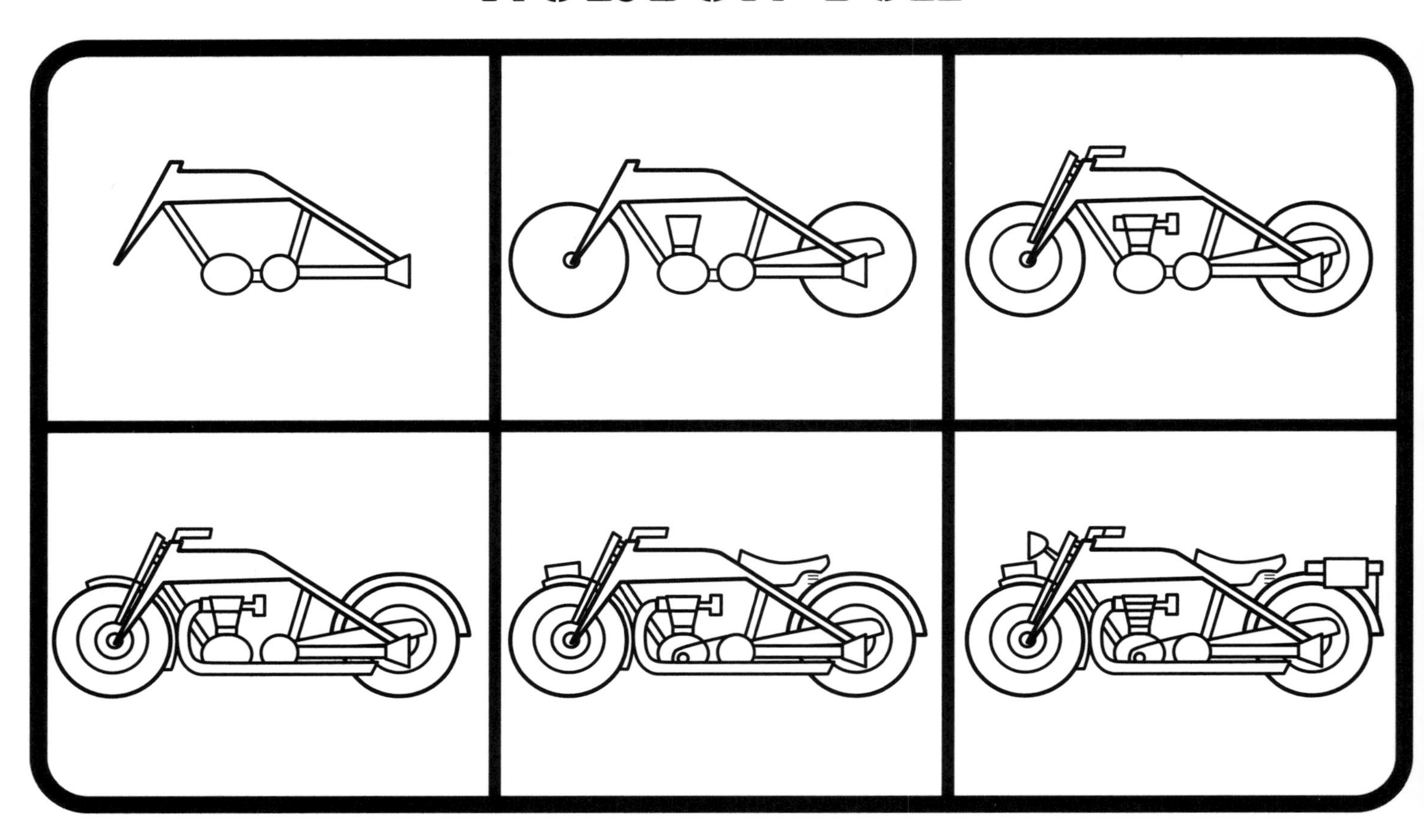

ZUNDAPP

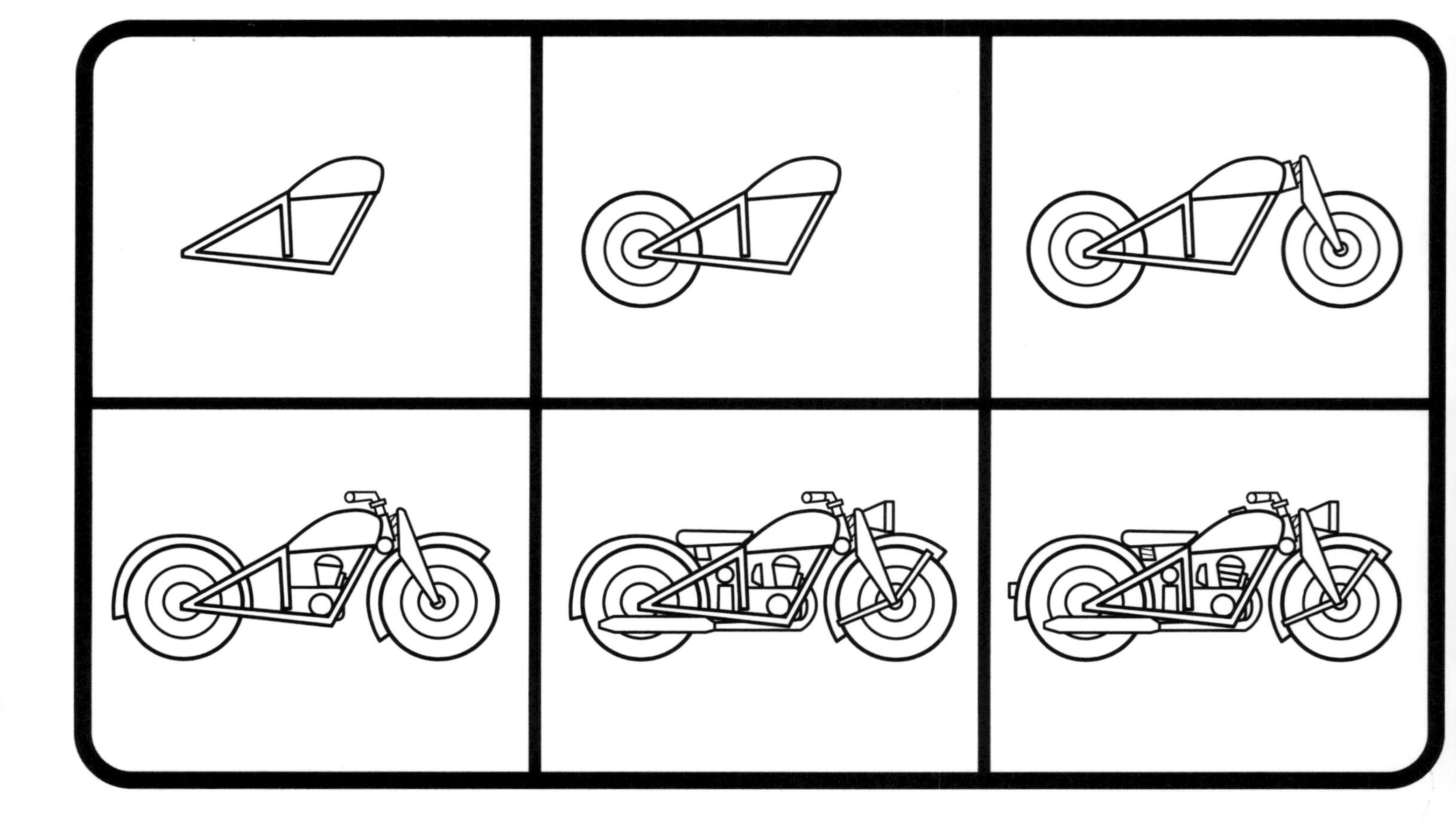

ARMORED VEHICLE

SUPPLY TRUCK

WILLYS MB JEEP

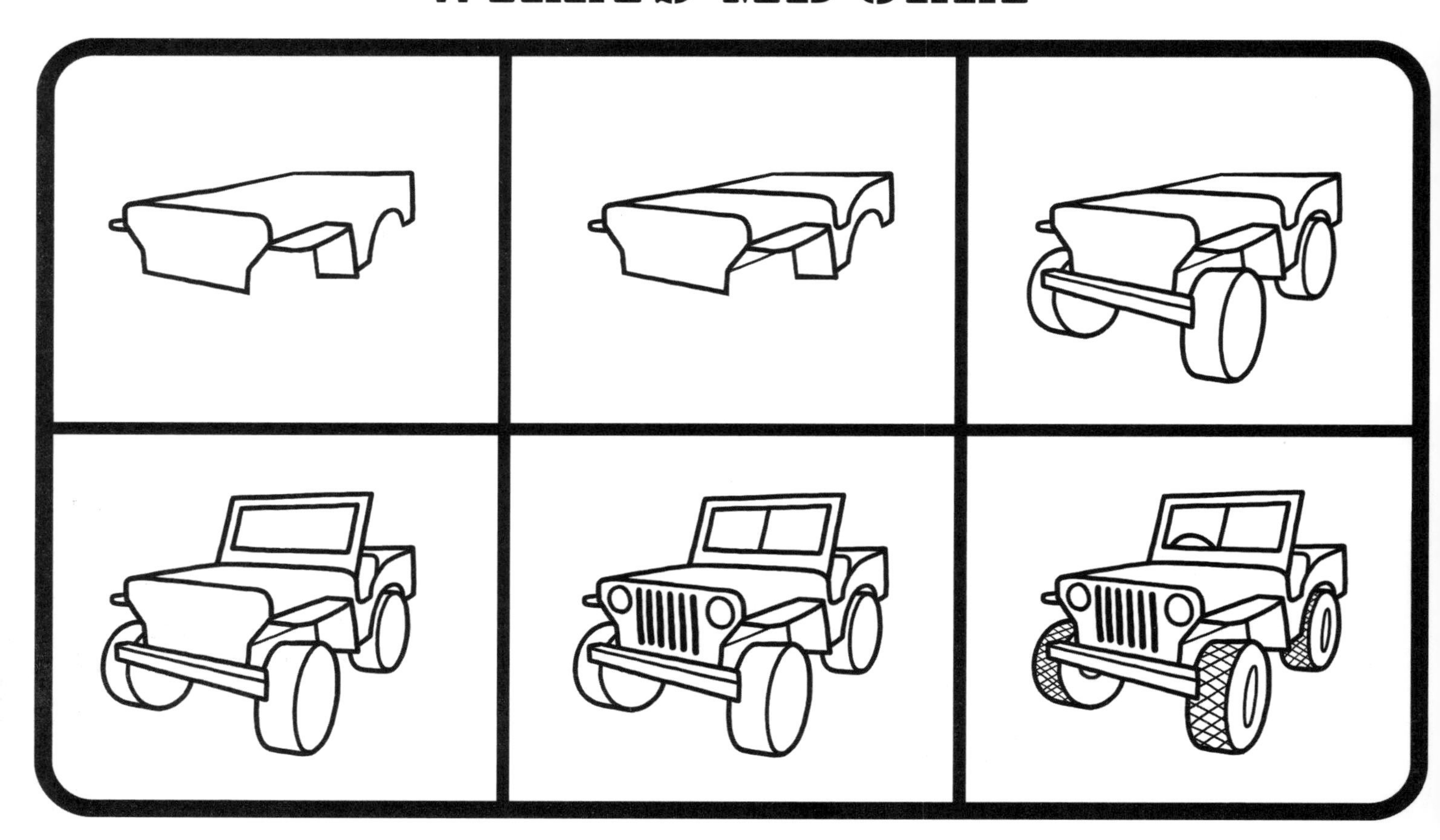

LIGHT STRIKE VEHICLE

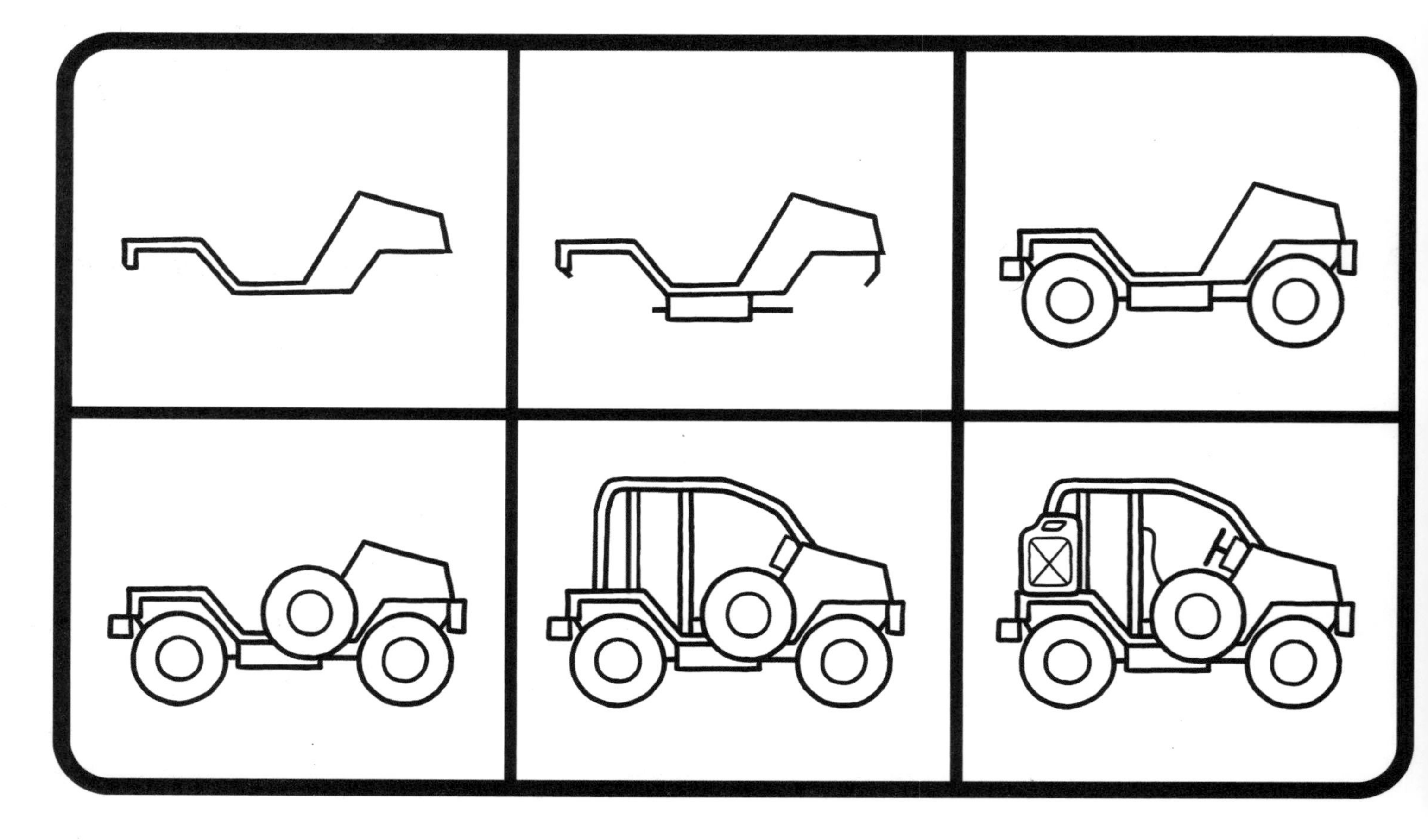

HUMVEE

MISSILE LAUNCHER

MLRS MISSILE LAUNCHER

AIR-CUSHIONED LANDING CRAFT

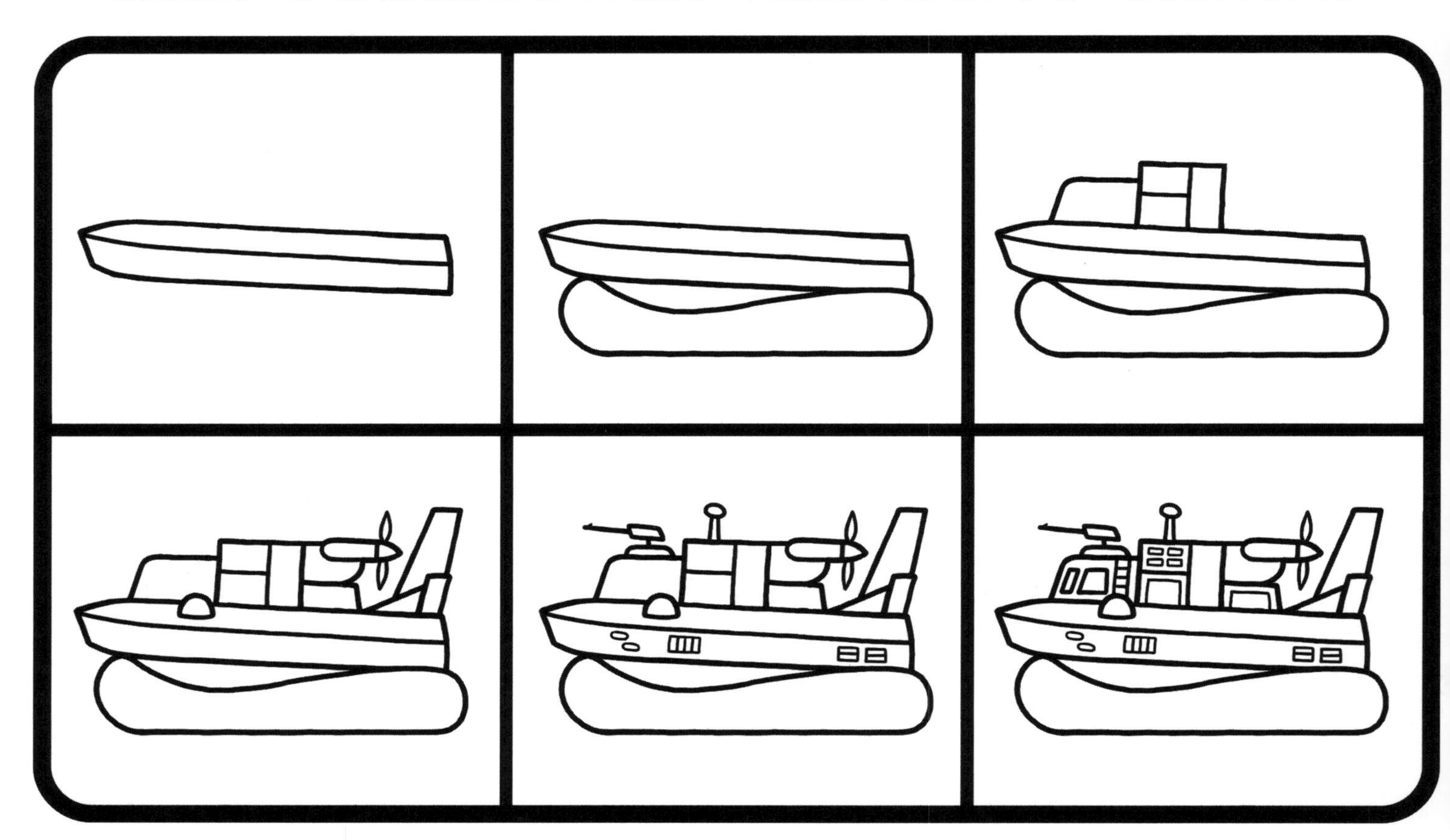

2400TD HOVERCRAFT

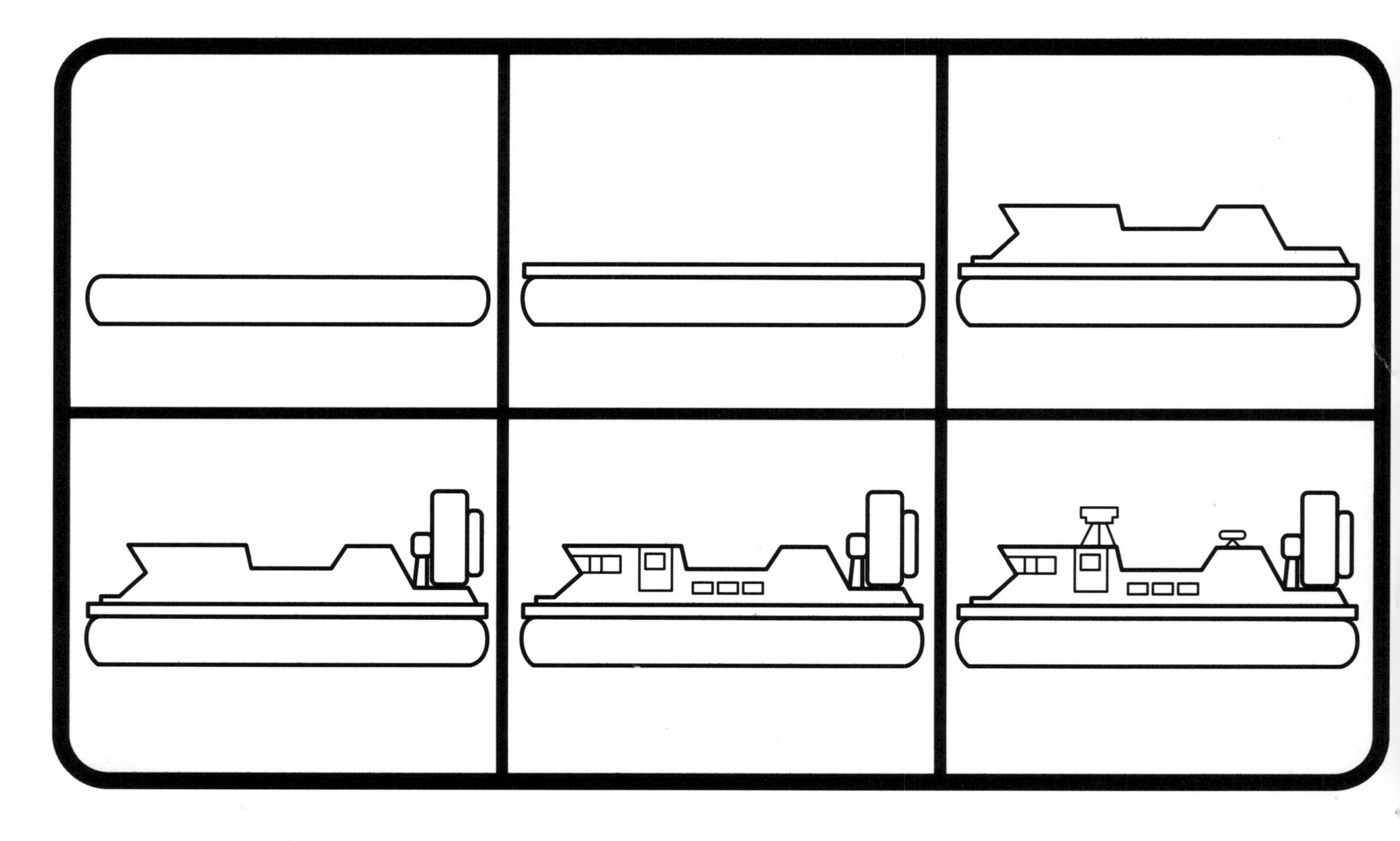

ZUBR CLASS HOVERCRAFT

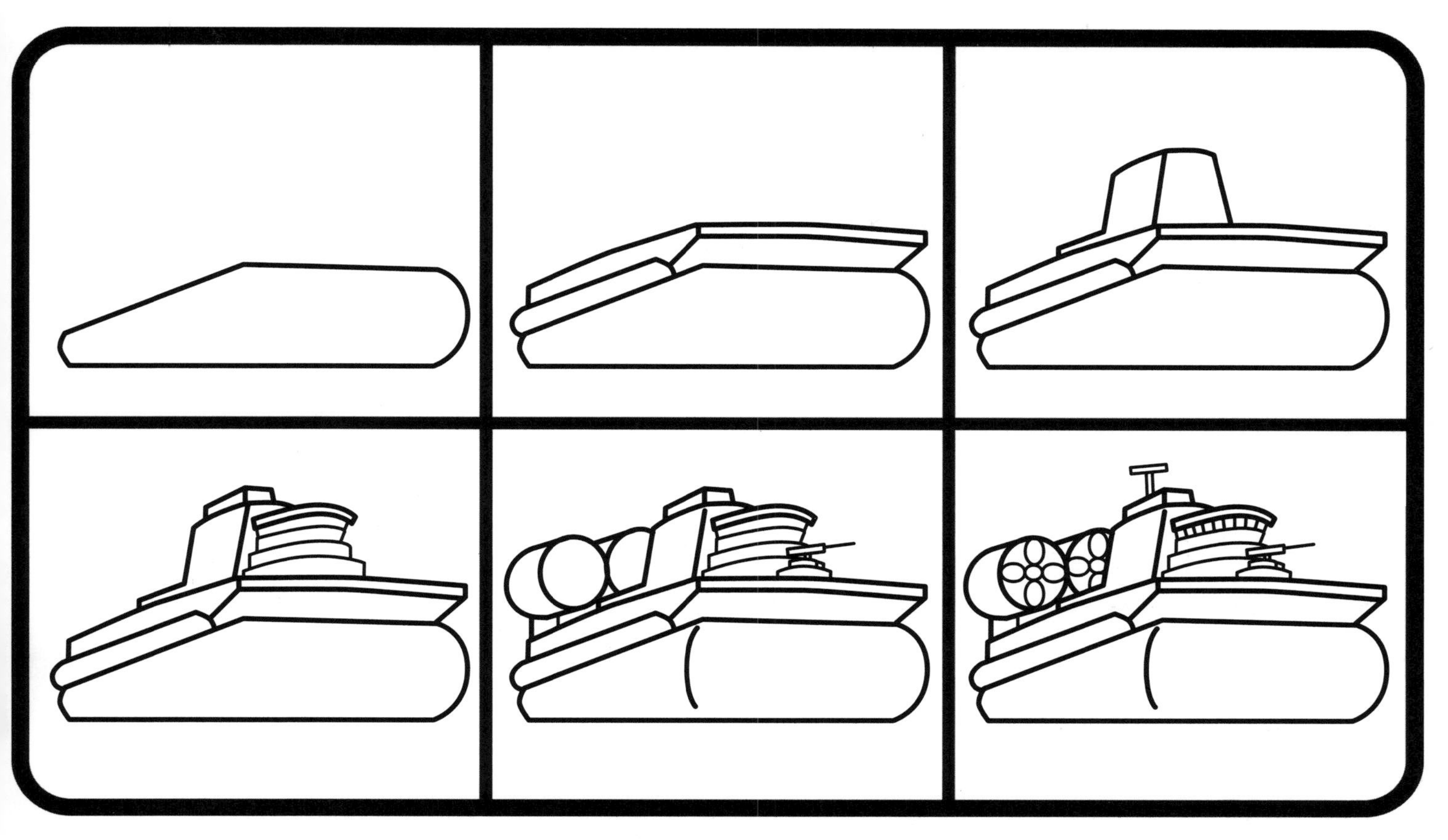

US COASTGUARD CUTTER

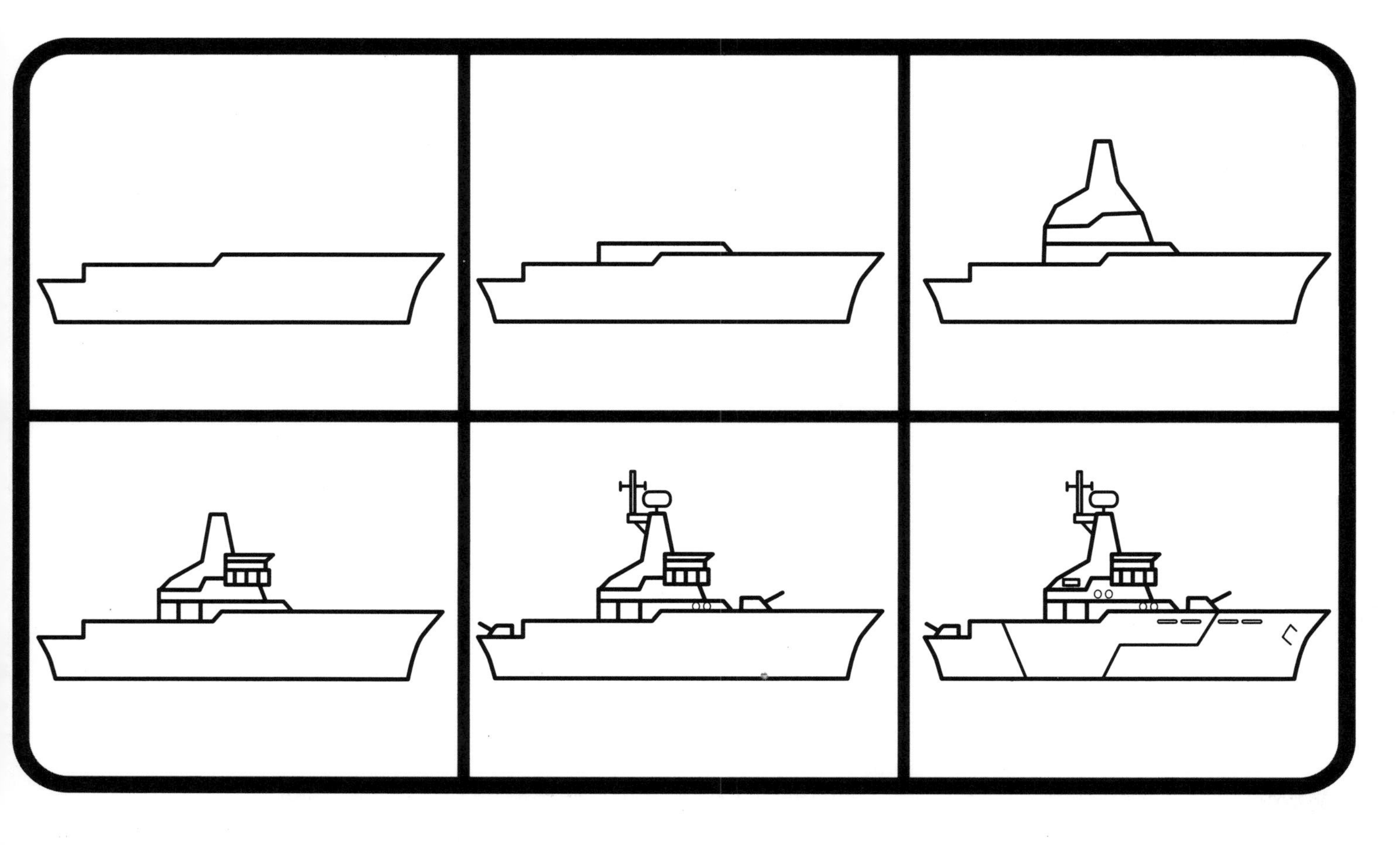

ARCHER CLASS TRAINING BOAT

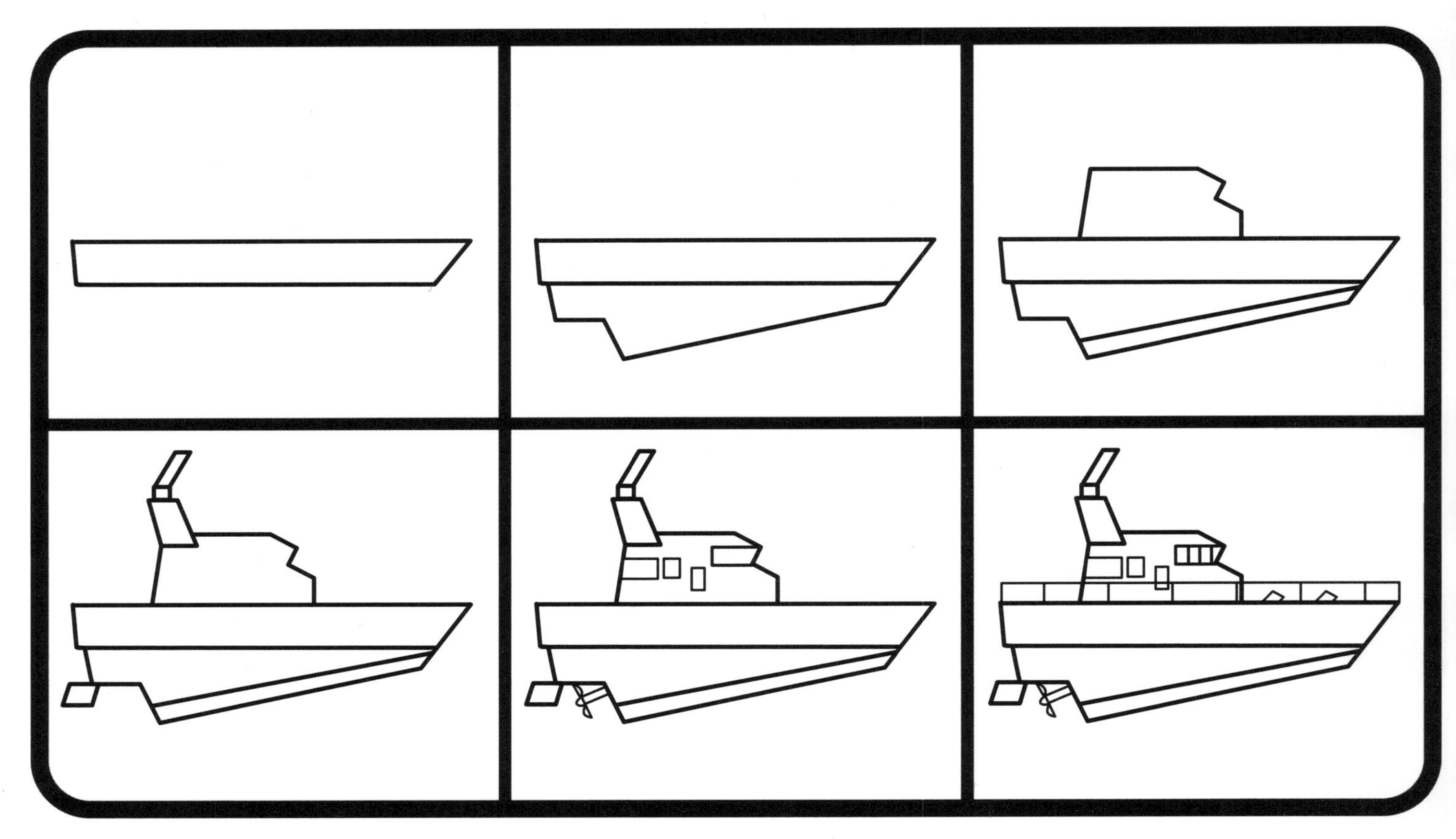

OFFSHORE PATROL VESSEL

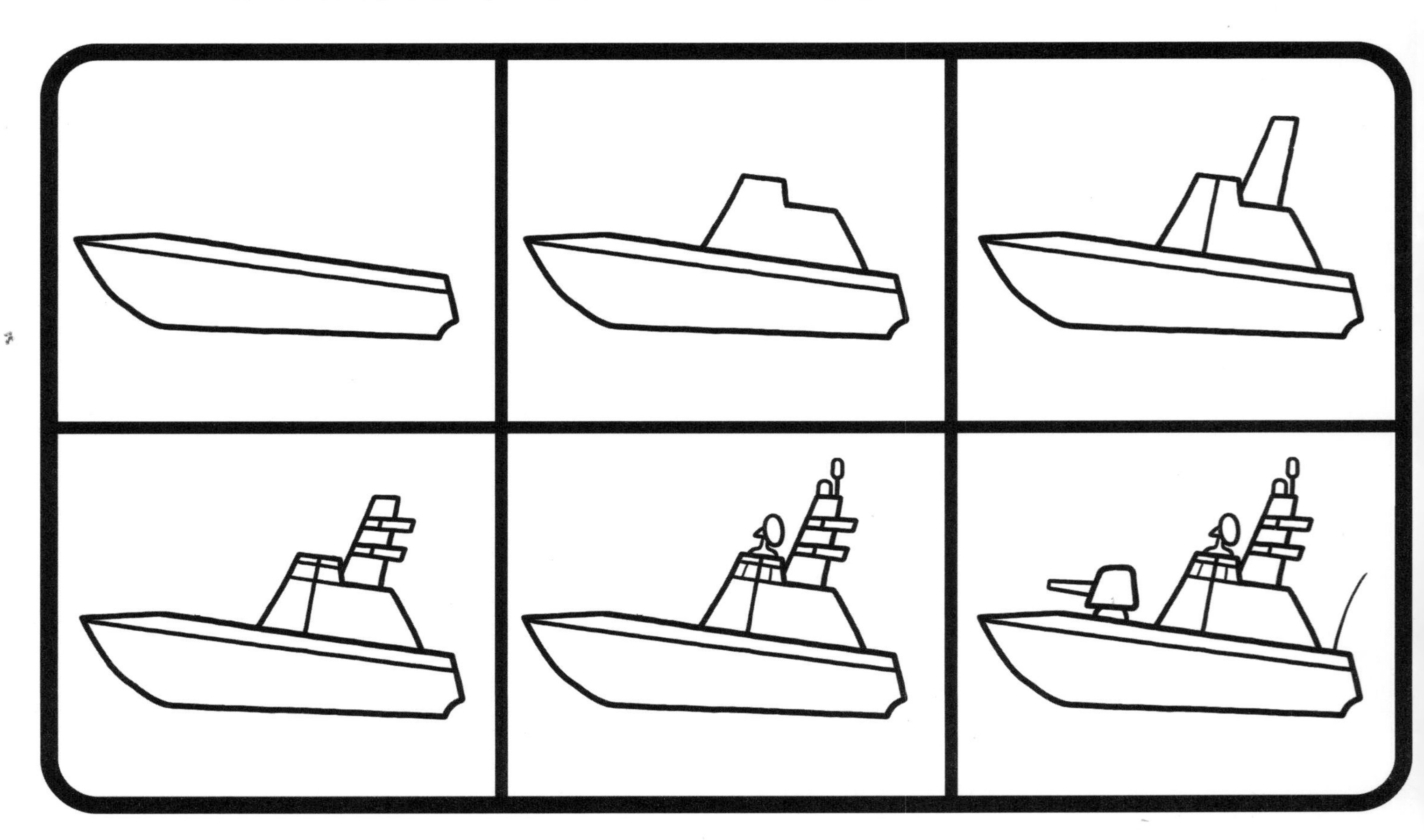